Stories for the Gathering

Stories
for the
Gathering

A TREASURY
FOR CHRISTIAN STORYTELLERS

William R. White

Augsburg
MINNEAPOLIS

To the people of Immanuel Lutheran Church,
Mt. Pleasant, Michigan

STORIES FOR THE GATHERING
A Treasury for Christian Storytellers

Scripture quotations, unless otherwise noted, are from the New Revised Standard Version Bible, copyright © 1989 by the division of Christian Education of the National Council of the Churches of Christ in the U.S.A. and used by permission.

The story "The Vision of Sir Launfall" is adapted from the book *Peace Be with You*, by Cornelia Lehn, copyright © 1980 by Faith & Life Press, and is used by permission. "A Second Chance" first appeared in the book *Fatal Attractions: Sermons on the Seven Deadly Sins*, by William R. White, copyright © 1992 by Abingdon Press, and is used by permission. "Two Funerals" and "The Holy Week Visitor," both by William R. White, first appeared in *Abingdon Preacher's Annual 1993*, copyright © 1993 by Abingdon Press, and are used by permission.

Cover illustration by RKB Studios, Inc.
Cover design by David Meyer
Text design by Ellen Maly

Library of Congress Cataloging-in-Publication Data

White, William R. (William Robert), 1939-
    Stories for the gathering : a treasury for Christian storytellers /
William R. White.
        p. cm.
        ISBN 0-8066-3345-X (alk. paper)
        1. Christian life. 2. Storytelling—Religious aspects—Christianity. I. Title.
BV4515.2.W47 1997
242—dc21   97-13007
                                                                                    CIP

The paper used in this publication meets the minimum requirements of American National Standard for Information Sciences—Permanence of Paper for Printed Library Materials, ANSI Z329.48-1984.

Manufactured in the U.S.A.   AF 9-3345

01   00   99   98   97   1   2   3   4   5   6   7   8   9   10

Contents

———•◦⟨∞⟩◦•———

Preface

A little more than twenty years ago my study of parables lead me to the conviction that if I was to be true to the message of Jesus I would have to learn to use the method of Jesus. I understood that Jesus had many options at his disposal. If the kingdom of God was a concept, Jesus would have lectured. If the kingdom of God was a doctrine, Jesus would have posted ideas to be absorbed. If the kingdom of God was a feeling Jesus would have used encounter group techniques to bring people together.

Of course the kingdom of God is not centered in ideas or feelings. It is centered in a person, Jesus himself. The kingdom of God is concrete and alive. To communicate the nature of this dynamic and personal reality, Jesus spoke in stories. It was the only method that could properly communicate his message.

I had long used stories to illustrate a point, but my discovery convinced me that I needed to tell stories and say with Jesus, "Whoever has ears, let them hear." For Jesus' stories do not illustrate a point: they are the point.

During my time as a camp director, I discovered that story was ideal for use by college counselors working with children and began to develop story-based material for Bible camps. It was just a few steps from summer camp to a Sunday school classroom, where I next turned my attention. I collected stories for teachers, and shared the wonder of story-*telling*, rather than story-*reading*. Three books grew out of those experiences, *Speaking in Stories*, *Stories for Telling*, and *Stories for the Journey*.

Recently I have turned my attention to the place of story in preaching. I have poured over the homiletical writings of Fred Craddock, Richard Jensen, David Buttrick, and Eugene Lowry to help me find my way. Lowry taught me to distinguish between story and narrative preaching.

In addition to preachers, I am indebted to two totally different sources, a radio program and a group of friends. Like countless other Americans I have spent many Saturday nights with my ear tuned to Garrison Keillor's "A Prairie Home Companion" on public radio. I have found his "News From Lake Wobegon," filled with stories of the joy and anguish of everyday life, a wonderful way to get ready for Sunday morning. The events of his mythical hometown are wrapped in grace. I began to wonder what would happen if rather than using a short story in a sermon on Sunday morning, the entire sermon was a story.

Late in September 1986, I decided to find out. After studying the assigned gospel carefully and spending far more time than usual writing, I came prepared with a story for my Michigan congregation that I thought addressed the biblical word. I began, tongue in cheek, by announcing that I had not had time to prepare a sermon. After listening to "A Prairie Home Companion" the night before, I decided to call my childhood home in Wisconsin for some news.

The "news" I shared was about a young man, Todd Ostrem, who lost his job after he was convicted of tax evasion, and subsequently couldn't get another job ("The Noon Bible Study"). The response was amazing and gratifying. Parents stopped me on the street or called me on the phone to tell me that their entire family talked in the car on the way home about offering people second chances. The next Sunday as I concluded the announcements, a vice-president of the local university raised his hand and asked with a smile on his face, "Is there any update on Todd Ostrem? Did he get a job?"

As time passed, and I told more "stories from back home," I discovered people could repeat the whole sermon months later. The week after Thanksgiving a young man in my confirmation class said, "Pastor, what you just said reminds me of Shark and Turk." When another lad in the class didn't recognize the names, he was informed they came from the Easter sermon the previous April ("Easter at the Boondocks"). When the boy said that he and his family had gone to Florida for Easter, the first boy, with help from two other classmates, told the entire story.

People were anxious to tell me what they found believable and meaningful in these story sermons. Their comments helped me form the character of David Zwanziger, the pastor who appears in most of the stories.

Television has long understood that if we are to be enticed to watch many hours of their programming, it will have to come in story form. Nearly everything that is aired—news, soaps, situation comedies, and movies are in the shape of narrative. Even the commercials.

Just as the great minds in the entertainment world continue to find new and vital ways to tell their stories, we in the church continue to find fresh ways to tell the old, old story of God's love and justice.

Stories For the Gathering includes seventeen longer stories that I wrote for worship, and subsequently rewrote for use in other gatherings, such as youth festivals, pastor's meetings, and lay training events. With the exception of "The Anniversary," a topical sermon which was written for a wedding, all are stories that grew out of my understanding of a particular text. The specific biblical references can be found in the index.

My greatest growth as a storyteller/preacher took place with the help of the people of Immanuel Lutheran Church, Mt. Pleasant, Michigan, where I practiced for fifteen years. Their love of story, and the great Storyteller, made me bold to attempt different ways to tell the good news of Jesus. I gratefully dedicate this book to them.

A few years ago, stores sold a poster that reminded us what happens when we treat a child negatively. The child who lives with criticism and rebuke, the poster said, grows up to be hesitant and fearful. I have long believed that a similar poster should be sent to congregations. Pastors who receive praise and encouragement approach the task of preaching with more enthusiasm and are willing to try new ways to announce the good news of God. Pastors who hear only critical words become tentative and cautious in their preaching. I believe congregations play a significant role in the development of their pastor, and often get the kind of preaching they deserve.

Part of the power and beauty of good stories is that they cross human barriers and appeal to people who live in different geographical and cultural settings. We don't have to live in rural Palestine and understand sheep to be touched by the biblical story of the Good Shepherd. The Danish tales of Hans Christian Andersen, the Russian stories of Leo Tolstoy, and the British stories of Beatrix Potter, for the most part, sound fresh and contemporary to American ears.

On occasion, the storyteller will find an aspect of the story time bound and will need to adapt the story to their own setting. Other times they will find that if they change the gender of a lead character, or the locale the story takes on a new urgency. Since traditional stories have already gone through numerous adaptions we can be free to tell them in new ways.

Still, most stories need no help from the storyteller. The stories in this book that take place in a small Wisconsin town have all been told to my Sunday morning urban audience. Listeners "translate" novels and TV stories from different cultures daily, and they can do the same with most of the stories in this book.

I am grateful to Walt Sutton, Marilyn Zorn, and the late George Zorn, who read portions of the text and offered criticisms. Many of these stories were first told to my best friend, and wife, Sally Lee White, an extraordinary elementary principal, whose uncommon common sense and encouragement, has been a gift to me for more than thirty-two years.

An Opening Parable

Some time ago Truth walked the streets of a large city dressed in plain, drab clothes. Whenever Truth talked to people it was with an icy intensity. At first people were fascinated with Truth, but never for long periods of time. People seldom invited Truth into their homes.

One day Truth saw Parable walking with a group of people. Parable, dressed spectacularly with bright clothes, wore a big smile. Truth waved to Parable and said, "I would like to talk with you, alone."

Parable waved the friends on and then stepped near a tree. "You look sad and out of sorts my friend," Parable said to Truth. "What is wrong?"

"Everything is wrong," Truth said. "I'm old and boring. People don't pay attention to me any more."

"I don't believe people ignore you because of age," Parable replied. "I'm as old as you are, and I have many friends. Let me make a suggestion. Lighten up, and brighten up. I'll lend you something to wear. You're bigger than I am, but with a little work I think I have something that might fit."

Truth took Parable's advice and dressed up in new clothing. The two began to spend time together. From that time on Truth and Parable have gone hand in hand. They make a wonderful pair.

CHAPTER I

Christmas
and
Other Festivals

The Reason *for the* Season

This story was written for Advent.

David Zwanziger was whistling as he came to work. He glanced quickly at the mail from the previous day, put "Selections from the Messiah," in his office tape deck, and began to read the lessons for the Second Sunday in Advent.

When he finished, he poured a cup of coffee and examined his appointment book. Like all Decembers, it was full. The Christmas season was difficult not only for many in the flock, but also for the shepherd. He learned this lesson his first December as a pastor, which was also his first December in Blackhawk, nearly seven years earlier.

David had expected the season to be like the Christmases of his youth. He remembered attending school plays, choir concerts, and family gatherings when he was a boy. He loved strolling through the small business section of his hometown listening to wonderful Christmas carols being broadcast over a tinny PA system for all the world to hear. Most of all he remembered church, a haven of peace and goodwill.

Rather than sailing through December on a sea of tranquility, however, he discovered that life in the pastor's office was more like tacking into a storm. His days were to be marked with stress, not peace. It all started when the month was but two days old and Dora Gilbertson marched into his office with fire in her eyes.

Tradition ran deep at Maple Street Lutheran. For fifteen years the Sunday school had put on the same pageant, "The Story of the Birth of Jesus Adapted from the Gospels," by Gertrude L. Allness. For ten years Gertrude had also directed the play. Upon Gertrude's death, her daughter Mary Lynn became the director. The year David arrived, Mary Lynn, who was eight and one-half months pregnant, reluctantly gave up the director's roll.

David, who had never seen the pageant or the script, was told by the Education Committee that he had to find a new director. One day when David was talking with Terri Jorenby, a woman new to both the community and the congregation, he mentioned his search. Terri, who had been in a couple of plays in high school, offered to direct.

The next week Terri met briefly with the Education Committee. "What do I need to know?" she asked.

One of the members quickly told her, "Mary is to be selected from the seventh grade class and Joseph from the ninth grade."

"Why?" Terri asked.

"Because we have always done it that way," was the reply.

During Sunday school the first week in December, Terri invited all the children who wanted a speaking part to read for her. Though she had seen several of the children in church, she didn't know any of them by name. For the part of Mary, Terri selected Alice Ann Isaacson. No one told her that Alice Ann was not a member of the church or that she was from a rough, crude family. No one told her that Dora Gilbertson had been in charge of costumes for eight years and assumed that her daughter Carme would be the next Mary. No one told David these things either, until Dora came to visit.

Dora entered David's office spitting mad. "How could the coveted role of Mary be given to an outsider?" she demanded to know. "Why was Carme passed over for the part? Why wasn't Terri told about the traditions of the church? Do you know anything about the Isaacson family? People in town say that Alice Ann can swear like a sailor. Is that the kind of person you want playing the part of Mary?" David grimaces to this day when he remembers Dora's visit. After listening quietly to Dora, David confessed that he knew very little about the pageant. He also told her that Terri's decision was final.

Two days after his encounter with Dora, Stephanie Hilboe called for an appointment. Stephanie and Tom had been married by David the previous spring. Stephanie arrived at his office in tears.

A native of Norway, Stephanie had met Tom at the University of Wisconsin when they were both students. Stephanie knew Tom and his family loved to hunt, but she didn't know it was his full-time occupation during November and December. She was not ready to be temporarily abandoned by her hunting husband. First he disappeared to hunt deer with his bow. Then he left for two weeks of firearms deer season, near the Michigan border. Just when she thought he had finally returned, he went for a weekend of musket hunting. It was too much!

Stephanie's visit was followed by Tom's visit. For David it was just one more painful event during the season of cheer. David had also discovered that a large number of men and women were anticipating their Christmas to be more blue than white. One by one they let him know that they were experiencing some form of depression. Most of the conversations that provided him with this information began when David greeted them in his normal way, "How's it going?"

One man responded by telling David, "Not so good. My father died a week before Christmas three years ago. Since that time I always get bummed out at Christmas."

A woman reacted in even stronger terms. "Horrible," she replied to David's greeting. "I'm single. This is a difficult time of the year to be alone. I really don't like Christmas."

David resolved to change his greeting the next time he saw someone, but the following day he forgot when his shopping cart nearly collided with one pushed by a first-year schoolteacher. "Hi, how's it going?" he asked.

She stopped and said, "Do you really want to know?"

For a moment David almost said, "No. I was just making small talk," but instead he stopped to listen. The woman told him she had become a teacher because she loved children. "Pastor," she said, "most people don't realize that children can be mean. I mean cruel." Moving her hand across her forehead she concluded, "I have had it up to here with kids." From that day on David only waved and greeted people nonverbally.

Meanwhile things grew worse with the Christmas pageant. Alice Ann Isaacson was slow to learn her lines. Carme Gilbertson, who had been cast as an angel but still hoped for the lead role, memorized Mary's part, as well as her own. Whenever Alice Ann stumbled, Carme prompted her in a loud sarcastic voice from back of the stage where the angels stood on a riser. Finally Alice Ann had enough. She marched back to the angel Carme, shook her fist, and spoke in a voice loud enough for everyone to hear, "The next time you open your yap, I'm going to punch your lights out!" The next morning Dora Gilbertson was in David's office again.

When Dora left, David thought seriously about asking the church council for a few weeks off. Had a pastor ever taken his vacation over Christmas, he wondered.

The next day when he was visiting some of his older parishioners at the Ebenezer Home, the director, Pastor Knute Lee, met him in the hall. "You don't have much of a bounce in your step," Knute observed.

"I haven't been witness to a lot of peace on earth and goodwill," David began. Knute immediately invited him to come into his office to talk. In the next few minutes David told his story, from beginning to end.

When he finished, Knute smiled and said, "Sin."

David was puzzled. "Sin?"

Knute nodded. "Sin. We think this season is about being nice. It isn't. Sin is the reason for the season. Most people sentimentalize Advent and Christmas, just as they sentimentalize children. They think children are nice and cute. They forget the little rascals are sinners. Sentimentalism in a first-year teacher can be dangerous. Kids can be charming, but they can also be mean and cruel.

"And marriage," Knute continued. "When people get married, most counselors don't focus on the sinful nature of the couple. I used to look both of them in the eye and say, 'What sin disturbs you the most about your spouse?' They would look at each other, bat their eyes at one another and coo, 'Pastor Lee, Charley is the most wonderful, loving man in the whole world.' When you are young and in love your brain often goes numb. Young married people need to realize that they are marrying a person who is in bondage to sin and cannot free themselves. Instead they seem surprised by sin."

Knute took a short breath and continued. "Yesterday I talked with my niece who just came back from a six-month teaching stint overseas. When she left last summer, she told me she was going to Thailand because 'Thai people are the most wonderful, kind, and gentle people in the world.' I asked her if there was a mutant strain that had been hidden from the rest of the society. 'If not,' I told her, 'you can expect those folks to be a lot like people everywhere else, wonderful in some ways, sinners in every way.' She came back a bit disillusioned."

David frowned. "Yours is a very gloomy view of the world."

Knute's eyes narrowed, "I prefer to think of it as realistic. And it is also biblical. Do you think God sent his Son to die because the world was wonderful, cute, and nice? Why is it that we forget that Jesus came to save the world from sin? Why is it that even pastors like you are surprised to discover their people are less than perfect? David, you still expect that Christmas is full of love and good cheer. That is a commercial fabrication. If people were 100 percent wonderful, we wouldn't need Christmas. It is because they are broken, depressed, and alienated that our message is needed."

"You are saying all this stuff is normal," David said.

"I am saying it is to be expected," Knute said. "It is also the reason we have Advent before we have Christmas. Advent is the period of preparation before the gift. Our society is so impatient that they jump right to Christmas, just as they prefer to go direct to forgiveness without the pain of repentance."

Knute thought for a moment. "Let me put it this way. Jesus is the main actor in the Christmas drama. Who is the main actor in the Advent drama?"

"We seem to spend a lot of time with John the Baptist."

Knute smiled. "Right. And what is the message of this gloomy ol' prophet? Repent! He tells people to turn around and head in God's direction. He is a vital part of this story because he helps us get ready to receive God's great gift. His message is the necessary preparation for the coming of the Christ child, and yet, when was the last time you saw anything about John the Baptist in our Christmas displays? I dare say never. Who wants to be reminded about sin and repentance? That is why so many churches begin to celebrate Christmas early in December. They are not doing their people a favor. They encourage people to ignore or hide from their sin. Since people experience the effects of sin—depression, anger, broken lives—they ought to have an opportunity to bring that to expression in worship."

Knute paused for a moment and finished gently, "David, be thankful for Advent, it is your opportunity to get people prepared to hear the wonderful story of God's love. First, remind them of their great need for God. Help them understand how they have sinned against God and their brothers and sisters. Then tell the story of the Savior and God's amazing grace as best you can. If you don't get them prepared in Advent, they won't hear the good news of Christmas. And David, don't be surprised when your people act like sinners. God isn't surprised. That is why he sent his Son."

David left the Ebenezer Home with a new resolve. Yet, she still wasn't through with the pain of Advent. Three days before the pageant, Dora Gilbertson scolded Alice Ann at rehearsal for not acting like a lady. Then she threatened her, saying, "I have half a notion not to make you a nice costume."

Alice Ann responded, "I won't wear anything you make anyway."

"You don't know how to sew," Dora said.

"No, but I know how to shop," Alice Ann retorted.

The next day she went to a secondhand store and bought an evening gown, complete with sequins, for three dollars. The night of the Christmas pageant, Alice Ann arrived dressed for a party. Dora objected that the dress didn't fit the part, but Terri said, "I don't think it's too bad. It certainly is an improvement over bathrobes."

Except for a few of Dora's friends, the congregation agreed that Alice Ann was stunning. Some even said she was the best Mary they had ever seen. Certainly she was the most memorable.

David finished his coffee, left his seven-year-old memories, and thought about the people in pain he would see the next couple of days. He knew that some would be distraught, others upset, and many more depressed. He also knew that they were hungry to hear about the gift of the Savior, God's response to the world's heartbreak. Next, David telephoned the new director of the Christmas pageant. She was young, just one year out of high school, but she did have experience with drama and had actually been in the pageant. When she answered he asked, "How did the first rehearsal go last night?"

The director told David there had been a minor scuffle between a couple of children in the cast and one of the fathers was unhappy with his son's part. "He wanted his boy to be a wise man, but I gave him the part of a shepherd," she explained. "I told him he could try out for the part of the wise man next year."

"It sounds to me like you handled it fine," David reassured her. "I have no doubt that you will do a great job. When is your next rehearsal?"

"Saturday," she answered.

"See you then, Alice Ann."

The Vision *of* Sir Launfal

This is one of many English stories that focuses on the Holy Grail, the legendary cup Jesus used the night of his betrayal. Although the ending takes place at Christmas, its emphasis on peace and service frees the storyteller to use the story for many other occasions.

Sir Launfal methodically went over his list for the third time. If he were to leave tomorrow on his great adventure, everything would have to be ready. He tested his sword carefully. It was sharp to the touch, and it gleamed when he held it up to the moonlight. Sir Launfal would use that sword with great courage against anyone who stood in his way.

Next, he checked his shield. The metal was polished, and the leather strap new and strong. He glanced toward the barn where his horse anticipated the journey. Sir Launfal had fed and curried him just moments ago.

Finally he knelt beside his bed to pray before he slept. "Dear Christ," he began, "tomorrow I begin my great journey in your name. I ask for your blessing and guidance as I search for the Holy Grail, the cup you used the last night you ate with your disciples. Make me pure, for only if I am pure will I be worthy to be the one who will find your holy cup."

When Sir Launfal fell asleep, he soon began to dream. His dream was so real that he actually thought it was morning and he was saying good-bye to all in the castle. Proudly he rode through the gates on his beautiful horse.

Just on the other side of the gates, however, a beggar stopped him. How annoying! At this high moment, at the start of his quest for the Holy Grail, he certainly could not be bothered with someone as un-important as a beggar. Disdainfully, Sir Launfal flung a penny in his direction and rode on.

Time can pass very quickly in a dream. Sir Launfal's dream covered many years. He searched everywhere for the Holy Grail. He fought many battles, but never did Christ even give him a glimpse of the cup he had used at the Last Supper before his suffering and death.

Sir Launfal was discouraged. He had become an old man, and in his dream he finally decided to return home. Sadly, he rode along the snow-covered road. As he came within sight of the castle, he saw all the lights ablaze, and he realized it was Christmas Eve. There would be much feasting and joy within the castle walls.

Sir Launfal rode up to the guard at the gate. To his dismay the guard did not recognize him. "No beggars allowed within the castle gates," he insisted and drove Sir Launfal away.

Sir Launfal was dejected. He got stiffly off his horse and sat down in the shelter of the castle wall. He looked at the light streaming out of the windows. It was Christmas Eve, the night the Christ child was born, and he was excluded from his own home. Had Christ rejected him altogether?

Finally the noble knight pulled his last crust of bread from his pocket. Just as he began to eat it, he noticed a beggar nearby. It was the same beggar he had seen at the gate many years ago as he was leaving on his mission. Sir Launfal broke his bread and gave half to the beggar. Then he went to the brook, broke the ice, and drew water for both of them to drink. As they ate together, and drank from the old knight's wooden bowl, a strange thing happened: Sir Launfal suddenly thought the crust tasted like fresh bread and the water like the finest wine! He turned to the beggar, but the beggar was gone. In his place he saw the shining presence of Christ. Then he heard Christ saying:

Not what we give, but what we share,
For the gift without the giver is bare;
Who gives himself with his alms feeds three—
Himself, his hungering neighbor, and me.

Sir Launfal looked down at his wooden bowl. It was no longer there. Instead, he held in his hand the Holy Grail. His search was over. With that the knight awoke from his sleep. It was morning. Sir Launfal believed Christ had spoken to him, and he knew what he must do.

"Put away my sword and armor," he instructed the servants. "I am not going to distant countries to look for the Holy Grail. It is right here in my own castle."

From that day on, Sir Launfal opened wide the gates of his castle to the poor and hungry. He welcomed both rich and poor alike and was friendly to all. In his castle all experienced the love and kindness of one who had supped with Christ.

Two Questions

Leo Tolstoy, who is best known for his novels, was also a writer of short stories. Many of these shorter works were inspired by Russian folktales and events in neighboring countries. This is my version of one of Tolstoy's stories.

There was once a king who felt the pressures and demands of his office. One day he said to his wife, "If only I could determine which people and which affairs of the kingdom were the most important, I could use my time better and thus be a more effective king."

"There are many wise people in the kingdom," the queen said. "Consult with them."

And he did. One by one, politicians, scholars, and advisers were invited to the palace to give advice to the king. Some suggested that his priests were most important. Others insisted that he focus his attention on the military, while still others urged him to give preference to the educators. Each argued hard and reasoned well. The king remained confused.

Once again he sought advice from the queen. "No two groups agree," the king told her. "How do I decide to whom I will listen?"

"Find a neutral party," she suggested. "Find someone who is not beholden to the military, the scholars, or the church. Perhaps it is time to visit the wise hermit."

The king agreed. Accompanied by his bodyguards, he set off to find the wise hermit who lived deep in the woods, a half day's journey from the palace. The hermit, it was rumored, would only receive the poor. Therefore the king put on humble clothing and before reaching the hermit's cell, got off his horse, left his bodyguards behind, and continued on foot alone.

When he reached the hut, the king saw the hermit digging a garden. The hermit paused long enough to greet the stranger and then proceeded to dig again. The hermit was thin and weak, and he breathed with difficulty as he plunged his spade into the earth.

The king approached the hermit and said, "I have come, my wise friend, to ask for answers to two questions: Which people are essential? Or to put it another way, with whom should I spend my time? My second question is, what affairs are most important, and should therefore be taken care of first?"

The hermit listened to the king intently. Then, without answering, he started digging again.

"You are tired," the king said. "Give me the spade. I'll work for you."

"Thank you," said the hermit, handing over the tool.

"After digging for nearly two hours, the king stopped and repeated his questions. The hermit did not answer, but stood up and reached for the spade saying, "You rest now; let me dig."

The king refused and continued to work. Two hours passed, and the sun began to set behind the trees when the king thrust the spade in the earth and said, "I came to you for an answer to my questions. If you can't or won't answer, say so, and I'll go home."

"Look," the hermit said. "Someone is running here. Let's see who it is."

The king looked to see a bearded man running out of the woods, clutching his hands to his stomach. Blood flowed between his fingers. He ran straight toward the king. Before he reached him he stumbled and fell to the ground moaning feebly.

Quickly the king and the hermit unfastened the man's clothing and discovered a large wound in his stomach. The king washed it as well as he could and bandaged it with his own handkerchief and one of the hermit's clean rags. When the blood kept flowing, the king removed the blood-soaked bandage, and then washed and bound the wound again several times.

Finally the flow of blood abated. The wounded man awoke and asked for water. The king brought fresh water and helped the man to drink it. Meanwhile, the sun had set and the air turned cool. The hermit and the king carried the wounded man into the hut and laid him on the bed. Then the king, exhausted from the unusual effort of the day, fell asleep.

When he awoke in the morning, the king looked up to see the bearded man lying on the bed, looking intently at him. It took a few moments for the king to remember where he was and the identity of the man in the bed.

"Forgive me," the bearded man said in a weak voice.

"I don't know you and have no reason to forgive you," said the king.

"I know you," the man confessed. "I swore to take vengeance on you for having executed my brother. I followed you to the home of the hermit and hid along the path, planning to kill you when you returned home. When several hours passed and you did not appear, I came out of my ambush to find you. I stumbled on your bodyguards, who recognized and wounded me. I escaped from them, but would have bled to death if you had not bandaged my wound. I wanted to kill you, but you saved my life. Now, if I live and if you wish, I will become your most faithful servant and order my family to do likewise. Forgive me."

Quickly the king made peace with his enemy, forgiving him and promising to send his personal physician to stay with him until he gained his health.

Leaving the wounded man, the king left the hut and looked for the hermit. He found him kneeling in the garden they had dug the day before. "For the last time, my friend, I ask you to answer my questions."

"But they have already been answered," the hermit replied.

"I don't understand," the king responded.

"If you had not been moved with compassion for my weakness yesterday and stayed to dig, you would have returned home. The man would have attacked you. I was the most important person, and the most important task was to do good for me. Later, when the man appeared, it was the best time for you to take care of him, for if he had died you would never have made peace with him. Therefore, he was the most important man, and what you did for him was the most important task.

"Remember this, there is only one important time: Now. And the most important person is the person we see now. God gives us one opportunity at a time. The person I meet now and the task that lies immediately before me are always more important than anyone or anything in the future. The future may never happen. The present is a reality."

Silent Christmas

This story has been adapted from several sources, including a fable by Leo Tolstoy and a German folktale.

The wife of a poor merchant died leaving him with five children, ranging from age six to fifteen. The older children assumed many of the household chores—cooking, cleaning, and helping the younger children.

When the merchant came home at night, he always brought a bag of groceries, food for the next day. After he set the bag on the table, he hugged each child.

Before they ate, he read from the scriptures, and prayed. Many nights, before bed, the children begged their father to sing with them. He frequently played his guitar and sang quiet folk tunes.

The first Christmas after his wife died the merchant said to his children, "This year there is not enough money to buy presents in the store. Instead, we'll all draw names, and you will make a present for one of your brothers or sisters. My gift to you will be a fine Christmas meal and a special song that I am writing. We will learn it in the weeks before Christmas and sing it in church on Christmas Eve."

True to his word, the father wrote a wonderful song of joy for the children, and began to teach it to them three weeks before the night of the Nativity. The children loved the song so much they sang it with great gusto and volume.

A rich man, who lived above the family, hated Christmas and hated music even more. Night after night he listened to the children sing the new Christmas song. It irritated him so much that he developed a plan to silence the singing.

Several days before Christmas he knocked on the door. "I have come to make you an offer," he said to the father, who listened carefully with his children standing behind him. "I will give you 100 gold coins if you promise not to sing for three months."

The father looked at the children. "That is more money than I can make in two years," he cried. "We will be able to buy presents for everyone in the entire family." The children cheered as the father accepted the bag of money, and the rich man's terms.

That night they began to plan silently how they would spend the money. The next evenings, after they ate, they sat quietly, reading and thinking. On the fourth night, one of the younger children said, "I'd rather have music than any stupid present. This isn't worth it."

One by one, the children agreed. So the father walked into the bedroom, retrieved the sack of money, and walked up the flight of stairs to return the bag to its owner. "We have discovered that there is something more important than money," he said. "I am sorry that our singing irritates you, but it fills us with joy. Our family can't imagine Christmas, or life itself, without music. When we sing we celebrate the best news that has ever been given poor people, that God so loved the world that he became one of us, living as a human being."

When the merchant rejoined his children he said, "We will learn to sing with greater feeling and less volume. In our joy we don't want to irritate our neighbor. What do you say to that?"

The oldest child spoke for them all, "We say let the music begin."

Song *of* Heaven

Many of our great hymns have a fascinating history.
This is one version of how "Silent Night," perhaps the world's
favorite Christmas carol, came to be written.

I'm afraid the news is not good," Franz Gruber said to his priest. "It is impossible to have the organ repaired in time for Christmas Eve services." The organist sighed, "We have less than forty-eight hours until we need it, and it will take over a week to get the necessary parts."

Father Joseph Mohr shook his head. "Christmas will not be the same without the organ leading our singing," he thought. The Festival of the Nativity was the high point of the year at the Church of St. Nicholas, located high in the Austrian Alps. "Do you have a plan?"

This time it was Franz Gruber who silently shook his head.

That night in 1818, Father Mohr went to see a play, based on the Nativity, performed by a group of touring actors. The audience, and especially Joseph Mohr, were deeply moved.

Rather than take his usual route home, the priest decided to hike up a hill that overlooked the village. As he stood gazing down on the houses, the village of Oberdorf was instantly transformed into Bethlehem. When he returned home the words to a poem took shape in his mind.

Silent night! Holy night!
All is calm, all is bright
Round yon Virgin Mother and Child!
Holy Infant so tender and mild.
Sleep in heavenly peace; sleep in heavenly peace.

The next morning he handed the words to his friend and organist, Franz Gruber. "See if you can wed these words to a melody," he said. The next afternoon, only hours before the Christmas Eve service, Gruber returned with a simple, lovely melody to the carol that was called "Song of Heaven." That night, with the organ standing in disrepair, Mohr and Gruber, accompanied by Gruber's guitar, sang for the first time what would one day be the world's most beloved Christmas carol.

A few days later Karl Mauracher, a well-known organ builder, arrived in Oberdorf to fix the ailing instrument. When he finished he invited the organist to try it out. Franz Gruber played several hymns, including the tune he wrote for Christmas Eve. Mauracher immediately asked permission to use it. "I'm certain folks where I live would love to sing it," he said.

Among those who learned the carol from the organ builder were the four Strasser children who sang for groups throughout the Zillertal Valley in the Austrian Tyrol. It quickly became a favorite of the children, and their audiences.

The fame of the golden voiced Strasser children spread beyond the area where they lived. They sang in concert halls, as well as in churches as far away as Leipzig. Finally, in 1832, they were invited to perform for the king and queen of Saxony. Their first offering was, "Song from Heaven." When they finished, there was nearly a minute of silence before they were greeted with thunderous applause.

The children sang many other songs that night, and for an encore sang the carol we now know as "Silent Night" again. From that time on, the song that was first sung in a remote Austrian village belonged to the world.

The Dale Starr Show

This was written for Transfiguration Sunday.

One Sunday, Evan Iverson told the people at church, "Next Friday will be the biggest day of my life."

Evan graduated from Titabawassee High School in mid-Michigan ten years ago. After staying home a year, he enrolled in a community college near Saginaw to study electronics. High school had not gone well for Evan. Many teachers thought his social skills impeded his learning.

The victim of a car accident at age three, Evan grew up with a metal brace on his leg and a chip on his shoulder. In grade school and junior high he answered every cruel joke, every taunt with his fists. In high school he became less combative, and more secluded. During his teen years, an insult about his disability created depression rather than anger.

When things didn't go any better in college than at Titabawassee High, he quit. Ashamed to move home, he found a job as a part-time custodian at St. Thomas Church. What appealed to him when he read the ad in the paper was the pastor's name, Garth Evans. Evan thought it was fate that they shared a nearly identical name.

In Pastor Evans, an older man whose wife died three years earlier, Evan found his first real friend. Each morning at exactly 10:15 the two drank coffee and talked. On Saturdays, when Pastor Evans finished his sermon, around 10:45, he stepped out in the hall and yelled, "It's donut-hole time," and the two men celebrated the end of the pastor's workweek with pastries, coffee, and a conversation that often lasted as long as two hours. During their Saturday morning celebration, Evan always asked, "What's the sermon about tomorrow?" The pastor then outlined what he had just written. This exercise seemed to serve both men well. Pastor Evans had an opportunity for oral rehearsal and Evan, who always sat out in the hall during the service, got a sneak preview of the next day's main attraction.

In addition to his job, there were two great loves in Evan's life, his train set and country western music. To accommodate his first hobby, he used the money left him by his late grandmother to buy a small house with a large garage on the north side of town. The two-story garage was turned into a train depot with a central dispatch and hundreds of feet of track. A neighbor painted the Michigan countryside on the walls, and he created rivers and hills to make the set more authentic. The operation became so large that it took at least three people to run it properly. To pay for his great passion, Evan took an evening job as a security officer at a local restaurant.

The second love of his life was directed primarily to the famous country balladeer Dale Starr. Evan purchased all of Dale Starr's albums and committed every lyric to memory. He decorated his entire bedroom with pictures of the tall singer who was known as "The man with the black curly hair."

Evan, normally a quiet man, was quite vocal about his taste in music. At St. Thomas he frequently cornered the organists and choir director to press his point. "This church would improve dramatically if we used a few Dale Starr songs," he insisted.

One September, Evan read that Dale Starr was coming to the Civic Auditorium in late winter. He not only wanted to attend the concert, he desperately desired to meet the great man. A week later he discovered that the Civic Auditorium needed a part-time janitor on weekends. Evan immediately quit his job at the restaurant and hired on. "Don't you see," he explained to Pastor Evans, "I'll have security clearance at the Civic and I'm almost certain to meet him. This is the chance of a lifetime. Years ago my father met the great Myron Florin, and to this day he hasn't stopped talking about it."

As the days to the concert grew shorter, Evan's speeches about his hero grew longer. Nearly every morning during the coffee break he recited the lyrics of at least one of Dale Starr's songs, many of which talked about friendship and love. On two different occasions he used the Sunday school's tape recorder to play his favorite tune, a tender ballad that told the tale of an old man who adopted a small, sick boy.

On the day of the concert, Evan was almost too excited to go to work. He left church at noon and arrived at the Civic Auditorium at four o'clock, two hours early and four hours before the concert began. His heart raced when he saw the big bus in the parking lot with "The Dale Starr Show" written across it.

After he punched the time clock, he made his way toward the space set aside for the singer. He was surprised to find only a handful of fans near the door. Evan had expected hundreds, perhaps thousands of people. He began to push a broom up and down the hallway outside the balladeer's dressing room. When he had cleaned the hallway eight or nine times, he decided to change the light bulbs, even those not burned out, hoping that the door would open and he would catch a glimpse of his hero. As he worked, Evan noticed that on different occasions the singer's manager brought girls into the dressing room. Around five o'clock Evan heard a loud noise, and a few seconds later the door flew open. "Hey, kid," the manager shouted, "we need a mop and a broom."

This was his big moment. Evan hurried over to the corner, filled a pail with water, and along with the requested items entered into what he considered the holy of holies.

The room was divided in half by a curtain that reached nearly to the floor. All Evan could see in the open half was a table and the manager. From behind the curtain that extended nearly the full length of the room, Evan saw smoke and heard girls giggling.

"Over here," the manager pointed. A pitcher had fallen to the floor, sending water and pieces of glass everywhere.

Slowly Evan began to sweep up the glass, while stealing looks in the direction of the giggles. Once, when his broom reached under the curtain to retrieve a broken piece of glass, an angry voice from behind the curtain told him to keep his broom on the other side. He had finished sweeping and had begun to mop up the water when he slipped, fell into the curtain, and bumped a chair on the other side. Suddenly he heard profanity. He turned around and saw his wavy haired hero, shirt off, glass in one hand, cigarette in the other, staring at him. "Who let this jerk into the room?" he roared.

Evan slowly walked across the room to pick up his pail. Once again the singer addressed him, "Get it in gear. Do your job and hobble outta here. Girls, come look at this pathetic little crip."

Dale Starr drew back the curtain and three girls giggled. The big star walked toward Evan and poured the contents of his drink on the floor. "Here is a little more you can clean up. Now get your butt moving."

Tears filled Evan's eyes. The insults triggered horrible memories. Before he could think, he grabbed the mop pail and flung the water with all his might at the singer. Then he put his hands on his hips as if to dare the larger man to retaliate. Instead, Starr stood stunned, wiping the water off his face. Moments later Evan's anger turned to unbelief. Down on the floor, floating on a sea of mop water, was a large piece of black wavy hair. The man was as bald as a glass bowl.

For a moment the girls stared incomprehensibly. Then as it all sank in they began to hang on to each other and giggle. Evan looked at the singer and the girls and began to laugh uncontrollably. Finally he walked out of the building, got in his car, and went home.

The next morning, right on schedule, Evan arrived at work with a bag of donut holes in hand. At coffee Pastor Evans, sensing something was wrong, waited for Evan to talk about his concert. Instead Evan asked his usual question, "What is the sermon about this week?"

"Well, I know what the text is, but for the first time in months I haven't completed the sermon by mid-morning Saturday. I don't know what to do with the assigned story."

Evan asked the pastor to explain.

"This Sunday we focus on what most people call the Transfiguration," he began. "Jesus takes three disciples up on a mountain where he meets Moses, the great lawgiver; and Elijah, the great prophet. The appearance of Jesus is changed and his clothes become as bright as a flash of lightning. While all this stuff is going on the disciples fall asleep! When they wake up Peter wants to treat each of the three great leaders the same, building each of them a shelter. Now here is the problem, the three men aren't the same. Only Jesus is changed. And when God speaks, he speaks only to Jesus—"This is my son, my chosen, listen to him!' This is a story about the uniqueness of Jesus."

Pastor Evans was gesturing wildly. "Jesus is the culmination of all that is taught in the Old Testament. Here is my question, should I speak about the glory of Jesus? People often get that all mixed up. They think glory is prestige. They think being great means being rich and riding around in a limousine. The greatness of Jesus is in his willingness to give himself, and to suffer. I guess that is why we read this story just before Lent." The pastor sighed. "The problem is, I've said all this before. I'd like something fresh."

The two men took a sip of coffee and nibbled on their last donut hole. "Perhaps," Evan began haltingly, "perhaps, you could talk about how eventually all our heroes fail us. Perhaps you could tell us how all of those we put on pedestals must be taken down—our parents, older siblings, sports stars, people we see on TV."

The pastor listened intently.

"Most of us have been disappointed in our life by someone we thought was important. I think you're right, we really do get mixed up about what it means to be great. We make people into gods, which is idolatry. Isn't this what the first commandment is all about? The only one who doesn't fail us is Jesus. The only one who teaches us the real meaning of greatness is Jesus."

Again the pastor nodded.

Evan got a little bolder. "You know pastor, we need to be reminded about these things all the time. Don't worry about repeating yourself. Now and then something happens that makes us ready to hear. We need to be reminded that the greatness of Jesus led him to the cross. We need to hear how compassion is greatness and how we see his compassion with the healing of the blind and curing of the lame. We need to hear that to be great is to be kind. Look at how he treated everybody with dignity; he cared about children and people with disabilities."

No one spoke for almost two minutes before Pastor Evans said, "You've been of great help, my friend."

"No problem," Evan said. He started to walk a few steps down the hall before he turned around. "It wouldn't hurt if you said something about the disciples falling asleep. I've got a feeling that God is often doing something right before our eyes and we're taking a nap. We miss what God is doing."

The pastor took out a pencil to jot down some ideas on a napkin. "Do you think I ought to tie this whole thing into Lent and the suffering of Jesus? I could tell how the greatness of Christ leads to his obedience and his suffering. I could urge people to use the forty days of Lent as a time to mimic Jesus. What do you think?"

Evan, hand on the door, shook his head. "Pastor, give me a break.

You're going to have to make some decisions yourself. I can't write the whole sermon for you. Besides, I gotta run to the music store. I thought I'd pick up something by this Bach guy you love so much."

Saint Sonja

Though I have told the story of Saint Sonja at several youth festivals, it was written for the Festival of All Saints.

Sonja Tollerud and Heidi Flugstad have been best friends since they learned to walk. Sonja is athletic and outgoing, Heidi quiet and studious. Sonja runs cross country, watches lots of TV, and loves sports. Heidi plays bassoon, reads classic novels, and prefers plays and concerts. Their parents, who operate adjacent farms, speculate that the girls are such good friends because they never compete against each other. They are different enough to admire the gifts of the other without envy.

Their differences are evident in temperament as well as interests. Heidi loved confirmation while Sonja treated it like a serious case of the zits. She didn't like memory work or going to class. Heidi treasured it as an opportunity to talk about God.

The day the confirmation class discussed the Sermon on the Mount, the two girls had a debate on the way home. Heidi was amazed with what she had just studied. "What Jesus is saying is that the sensitive, the caring, the empathetic are those who are most like God."

"Get real," Sonja countered. "What he says is, blessed are the wimps! Can you imagine being the kind of person he describes— meek and pure in heart. Give me a break. The world chews up those kinds of people."

"I don't think you can call someone who opposes injustice, who helps feed the hungry, or who puts their life on the line for peace, a wimp," Heidi protested. The debate was never settled, rather it continued in a different form when they entered high school.

During her junior year Sonja developed a huge crush on Mr. Preston, the gym teacher and JV basketball coach. "Have you ever seen muscles like his?" she cooed to Heidi one day. "He looks so neat driving his white sports car. About the only negative thing about the man," she confided, "is that he is married."

For months Sonja gave Heidi daily reports of the life and times of Mr. Preston. She retold stories he shared about his college football exploits. She just loved the way he coached the basketball team. "A coach has to chew out his players in order to get the best out of them," she told Heidi.

"I don't know," her friend replied. "There is something about the man I don't like. He seems so self-centered. And he doesn't treat people, particularly girls, with respect."

"Heidi," Sonja said shaking her head, "I believe you are sounding more like Mrs. Larson every day."

Heidi smiled. It was true that she had been influenced by Mrs. Larson, a wonderful English teacher who was well known for her concerns about violence and war. Heidi's time with Mrs. Larson and her husband extended beyond the school day when she baby-sat for the Larson's three children. It was hard not to be influenced by someone so brilliant and sensitive.

Just when it seemed that nothing could stand in the way of the girls' friendship, Sonja began to hang around with Brad Peterson and a group of his friends. Heidi wasn't impressed with Brad and thought he and his buddies were too loud and too crude. The more Sonja hung around with her new companions, the more Heidi faded into the background.

One day Sonja decided to run home rather than to practice with the cross country team. The coach gave her approval since the distance to the Tollerud farm was about what she would run with the squad, and it saved her parents a trip into town. Sonja changed her clothes in the locker room, put them in a bag and gave them to Heidi to drop off at her house.

Sonja's plan was to run south through the old stone quarry, cut across an open field and head west down County Trunk D. It was more scenic than running around the city, and she could also avoid cars and dogs, a runner's plague.

As she ran down the stone quarry road her face lit up. Ahead was Mr. Preston's white sports car. Would he see her running? She stopped, took a couple deep breaths, and then ran with as much power and grace as she could, given the perspiration running down her face.

When she reached the car she could see that it was empty. She paused a moment and headed up the old foot path to the top of the quarry. When she reached the peak she saw her idol passionately kissing his wife under a gigantic oak. "How romantic," Sonja thought, and kept running. But there was a loud crack when she stepped on a branch. Mr. Preston whirled around and demanded, "Who's there?"

Sonja stopped, smiled, and shouted, "It's only me, Mr. Preston. I'm just . . . " Her voice dropped when she discovered the woman with him was not Mrs. Preston. She panicked and fled across the open field as fast as she could go. She ran powered by anger, embarrassment, and shame.

It was three days before she told anyone. Heidi was wonderful. She listened quietly and didn't even say, "I told you so." The next few days the girls again spent a lot of time together.

The following Monday, Halloween, Sonja invited Heidi to go trick or treating. "A whole bunch of us are going. It'll be just like when we were kids. I'm going to dress like a witch. I've got a big pointed black hat, a black dress, and I'm going to carry a broom. Brad Peterson is going to drive."

Heidi quickly refused. "I don't want to get involved with those kids," she told Sonja. "I don't trust them." Normally Sonja would have teased Heidi about being square, but this time she had a few doubts herself.

Brad arrived thirty minutes late, his car full of clowns, ghosts, and other costumed creatures. Sonja managed to cram herself into the front seat, big hat, broom and all. The car headed east toward town before turning south, down a dark side road, less than a mile from Sonja's house. Brad parked the car just off the road. Everyone got out. "What's happening?" Sonja asked.

One of the guys who was opening the trunk laughed. "We're going to loosen up a bit. You might call it the pre-game warm up."

Inside the trunk was a case of beer and several bottles of liquor. The bottles and cans were opened quickly and the drinking began. Sonja was the only non-participant. In a few minutes Brad walked over and offered her his bottle. She shook her head. "Come on, Sonja, loosen up."

"Brad, I didn't know people were going to drink."

"So what?"

"I don't like it. I don't think it's right."

Brad exploded. "Don't think it's right. What are you, a blooming saint? Hey folks, I'd like you to meet Saint Sonja. She may dress like a witch, but she is really a saint." The group cheered.

Another boy joined in, "Hey, that's got a ring to it. Saint Sonja."

Before Brad could say more, Sonja, with loud laughter and jeers behind her, took off. For the second time in three weeks she ran home, frightened and embarrassed. Only this time she ran with one hand on her witch's hat and the other carrying a broom. Under different circumstances she might have found this funny. Not tonight.

When she reached the house, she tore open the door, and ran in the living room. Before her startled parents could speak, she cried, "Don't even ask," and went straight to her bedroom.

The next morning the school was buzzing. A new house under construction had been vandalized the night before. Someone had torn down the rafters and destroyed a wall with beer bottles. The police suspected teenagers. Sonja was sure she could identify the group. Before the day was over, classmates confirmed her hunch.

On Thursday night, her emotions still bruised, Sonja asked Heidi for a ride to choir. Heidi was surprised. Sonja hadn't sung in choir for over a year. On the way Sonja told her old friend what had happened. "I hope Pastor David will talk with me for a minute after choir," she said. When they got to church they found out that the pastor was out of town. "Would it help to talk to Mrs. Larson?" Heidi inquired.

Sonja thought for a moment. It would.

Immediately after choir the two girls went to the lounge with the teacher. Before Sonja sat down, she demanded, "What do you do with the stuff I tell you?"

Mrs. Larson smiled. "Everything you say in this room will be held in strictest confidence. You can be sure of that."

Sonja took a deep breath, looked at Heidi and started to tell her story. She began by telling how she discovered this "unnamed" man, a man she greatly admired, in the quarry with a woman other than his wife, and she followed with the events of Halloween night. And then she broke into tears and cried, "This guy called me a saint! Just because I wouldn't drink; he called me a saint in front of the whole group. It was so embarrassing."

Mrs. Larson smiled and said, "I think he may be right."

"Well, thanks a lot."

"Sonja, do you believe that Jesus Christ is your Lord and Savior?"

She bristled. "What is this, another confirmation quiz? Of course I believe in Christ. I made my confession, didn't I?"

"You did. And that makes you a saint. A saint is not someone who is perfect. A saint isn't a goody-goody. A saint is a believer. Paul begins his letters by writing, 'To all the saints in Christ Jesus who are at . . .' He meant 'to all the believers.' One of the clear implications of that confession is that believers accept a code of behavior different from many in the world. The reason that you are upset with your married friend is that you believe the promises he made at his wedding are sacred, and you don't need alcohol to enjoy yourself. You know alcohol and gasoline is a killer. Sonja, that young man didn't know that he was paying you a compliment."

"It is just that being a saint sounds wimpy."

Mrs. Larson continued, "When I was young all my heroes were big and strong. Now my heroes are still strong, but they are people who are strong on the inside. One of my heroes is your Aunt Catherine who has raised a child with Down's Syndrome by herself after her husband died. Another hero is Mr. Krohn, the janitor, who finds homes for foster children. Still another hero is Mrs. Thompson, a five-foot giant who works fifteen hours a week at a shelter for abused women. My heroes are people who help the sick or feed the hungry. I really believe that the blessed of the world are those who are merciful and poor in spirit."

Heidi moved next to her best friend, put her arm around her, and said, "Sonja, I love you. And I think you are a saint. Remember the Sermon on the Mount that we argued about. Well, it talks about you."

Sonja bristled, "What do you mean?"

"It says, 'Blessed are those who are persecuted for righteousness' sake, for theirs is the kingdom of heaven.' You have gone through some tough times because of your convictions. You stood by your principles even when others ridiculed you. That doesn't sound like a wimp to me. That sounds like something only the brave would do."

When they left that night Sonja appeared relieved, if unconvinced. Both girls were quiet as the car wound it way down County Trunk D toward the farms. About a half mile from home, Sonja asked Heidi to stop the car. After she turned off the radio, she began to sing. Soon Heidi added her mellow alto, a big grin on her face. The words found their way out of the open window, into the cool night air:

> *Oh when the saints, go marching in,*
> *oh when the saints go marching in,*
> *O Lord I want to be in that number,*
> *when the saints go marching in.*

Lift Up Your Hearts

"Lift Up Your Hearts" was first told at an ecumenical Thanksgiving service.

Life is never dull when my friend Rex drops by the office to talk. The other day when he was sitting on the couch I asked him, "What is the best thing about living to be eighty-four?"

"You know you've finally grown up," he said, quick as a whistle.

I laughed.

"That's the trouble with you, White" (he never calls me by my first name), "you can't tell when a man is serious. When you're young you use up a lot of your energy on worthless feelings. A lot on fear.

That's natural. When you're young you still don't know what will hurt you and what won't. Jesus told folks not to fear those that kill the body, but rather those who can kill the soul. Most people don't fear soul death until they're past forty. Then there is envy. The young expend a lot of energy on envy."

"I'll bet you didn't spend much time with envy," I offered.

"Not true," Rex countered. "Like most everyone I envied 'ol Bill Burkhart and his 'Midas touch' for maybe twenty years. He'd stop by the shop in a shiny new car and complain about how hard it was to be rich. 'Why, I paid more in taxes this year than my daddy ever made,' he'd say. Then he would lift his arms up so we could see his jewelry. Everybody in the barber shop would look at ol' Bill wide eyed and amazed. It'd take us two days before we stopped wishing we was him. When you get to eighty-four you put a lot of things in perspective."

"You no longer want to be rich?" I asked.

"Being rich ain't worth a bucket of warm spit," Rex bellowed. "Course being poor isn't anything to stand in line for either, but at eighty-four who would change their life for that of ol' Bill? Nobody I know. His kids became outlaws, his wife took to drinking, and he has that dull look about him that you see with folks on 'Lifestyles of the Rich and Famous.' Even when they smile they all look sad."

"Why are you always so hard on the wealthy? I demanded.

"Because wealth numbs you."

"I'm confused," I said. "What do you mean?"

"Wealth numbs you," Rex repeated. "It dulls your senses. First thing is you can't see well. The more money you get the fewer free things you see, like sunsets or the face of a puppy dog or the beauty of morning fog lifting off a stream. They think the only thing worth seeing is what they can buy—fancy new cars, plush furniture. Their hearing gets numbed too. Rich folks don't hear birds sing or take time to listen to nature's voices. Have you ever noticed how many people walk around town with earphones on. It's sad. Course I always figured the reason the rich don't hear is that cash registers make 'em deaf."

Rex made a sound like a cash register. "But most of all, money seems to numb people to God. They think they've earned their way in the world. They forget to say thank you and soon they forget to thank God."

Rex paused. "You remember that Maslow fellow?"

I smiled. Rex didn't often give me much time to talk, so I decided to strut my stuff. "Yes, among other things he developed a hierarchy of needs. He said our lowest need was physical and that the greatest need was love and self- realization."

"Right," Rex replied, "and not a bad job as far as he went."

I was astonished. "You think you can improve on Maslow?"

"Any good Calvinist can improve on Maslow. Just answer the first question in the Westminster Catechism. 'What is the chief end of human life?' Answer: 'To glorify God and enjoy him forever.' Are you still reading Scripture, White?"

"Thanks for the sarcasm, Rex," I replied.

"Well, the whole Bible moves by doxology. 'Who is like thee, O Lord,' or 'There is none like Thee, O Lord,' runs through the whole of Scripture. What does it tell you? It tells me that our highest need is God. Our greatest need is to live with a sense of awe and wonder. To be fully human we have to praise the almighty and have a heart overflowing with thanks. That is our greatest need."

He wasn't done. "Show me a man or woman who doesn't say Wow! at least once a day and I'll show you a person whose soul will soon dry up like a raisin. If I were a doctor I'd tell half my patients to skip the medicine and go out and ponder the mystery of an oak tree. And then I'd have 'em make a list of all the things they got by sheer grace, like the color of their eyes and their health. Finally I'd ask them to make a short list of the people who touched their lives. Then with the money they normally use on pills, call 'em up and thank 'em. I don't suppose Blue Cross would cover it, but it would do a lot more good. A grateful heart is the best medicine in the world. That's why you church folks are healers—worship is therapeutic."

Suddenly I remembered something I wanted to clear up. "Speaking about grateful," I said, "I'd like you to explain why you were so tough on that Jamison fellow last week."

About six weeks ago a man stumbled into my office all liquored up. He said he needed help in order to stop drinking. I spent the best part of the day getting him to detoxification and then another day or two helping his family get squared away. I called Rex, who with some buddies from Alcoholics Anonymous, visited Jamison. We helped him through the program. Later, Rex asked me if Jamison had kept in touch after he finished rehabilitation. I shook my head. Then he asked if Jamison had called to say thanks. I said, "Rex, I'm a pastor. He doesn't need to pat me on the back for everything I do for him. I was only doing what any pastor would do."

Well, Rex stomped by me and without asking picked up the phone and called Jamison. He proceeded to read the poor man the riot act. I was amazed at the whole process. When he finished the conversation he threw up his hands and walked out the door. This was my chance to find out what happened.

"I'm about to give up on you ministers," Rex said shaking his head. "You think I wanted him to thank you in order to make you feel good? You don't need the thanks, but the man needs to say it. He can't live without thanksgiving. Part of his drinking problem is that he doesn't know how to be grateful. He has a social illness and a part of the cure is gratitude."

Rex picked up a Bible off my desk. "You remember that story about the ten lepers who were cleansed?"

"Remember it," I said, "I'm preaching on it Thanksgiving Eve."

"You probably don't even understand it," Rex sighed. "Leprosy is another social illness. It not only damaged the skin it shrunk the spirit. People got to feeling sorry for themselves and they forgot what there was in life to be thankful for. Praise, thanksgiving, makes the human spirit grow. It expands the self, the person. When those nine fellers failed to come back Jesus knew that the skin may have cleared up, but not the spirit. It was still shrunk and distorted."

"The only man who returned to thank Jesus was a foreigner," I commented.

"That's St. Luke's reminder that the world is full of surprises. The great hymns of praise come from some of the most unlikely places. I remember ol' Tommy Olson, a man who slid around town on his knees, pushing a little cart with his arms, selling homemade soap. People said it not only took off grease but also the first layer of skin. Tommy was forever saying, "We often forget how fortunate we are," and meaning it. Lou Gehrig, pride of the Yankees, amazed everyone when he was suffering from that lateral sclerosis thing by not being bitter. There wasn't a dry eye in the place when he stood before the crowd in

New York, just before he died, and said, 'Some have said I've had a bad break, but I have a wonderful wife, great friends and have played before thankful fans. I consider myself the luckiest man in the world.'"

Rex had almost talked himself into tears. He dabbed at his eyes with a handkerchief and continued. "Many people who have been given the most have sour spirits. Others who seem to have less live with an anthem on their lips and a doxology in their hearts. I ask you, what is more valuable, a grateful spirit or a big bank account?"

Rex put the Bible back on my desk. "You want to know about the sadness of youth? They have health, strength, clear vision, and they don't even know how lucky they are. Many of them moan and groan more than a herd of cattle. Not until some gifts are taken away do they see what they have. Is that sad or what?"

I began to excuse myself. "I've got a sermon to write," I said.

"You know the real vision of the Samaritan leper don't you?"

I said, "I think so."

Rex didn't wait for my answer. "He saw the giver behind the gift. He was able to see the hand of God working through Jesus. Ultimately that is the test of sight, to be able to see God working in the world. He is hidden you know. People cry out to see God face to face, but they couldn't handle that. Instead, God works in other ways. Faith is being able to identify the giver and not just the gift. The next part is to lift up your hearts. I think that part of the communion liturgy where we sing, 'Lift up your hearts' and the congregation sings back, 'We lift them to the Lord,' is about the most profound thing I know."

Rex walked to the door. "Just one more thing," he said. "Are you going to use any of this in you sermon?"

"Probably," I admitted.

"Well?"

"Well what?"

"Well?"

"Oh," I said, finally catching on. "Thank you."

Rex smiled. "That's more like it."

As he walked out the door he turned and winked, "Lift up your hearts."

I watched him get into his car and as he drove away. Then I said quietly, "We lift them to the Lord."

No Big Deal

". . . if we have died with Christ, we believe that we
shall also live with him" (Romans 6:8).

Mary Lawson, a first-year seminary student, spent part of January working with Pastor David Zwanziger. Like all first-year students at her seminary, she spent three weeks understanding ministry from the point of view of a parish pastor. One of her most memorable experiences was observing David preparing adults for Baptism. At one of the last sessions, Mary was surprised when David told the class, "Baptism is serious business. You are inviting the Spirit of God into your lives. Often the Spirit makes dramatic changes. What you are about to experience is nothing less than rebirth. You may never be the same again."

After the class Mary said, "I haven't heard people talk like this in seminary. Did you learn this from a seminary professor?"

"No," David responded. "I learned about Baptism from my mechanic."

When Mary asked David to explain he began to tell her about Janice and Loren Getter. "It all started," David said, "about four years ago when Janice, an active member of the church, walked into my office. My life is a mess," she cried. "I'm twenty-five and I'm raising four children."

David was puzzled. "I thought you had three girls."

"I'm counting my husband, Loren," she replied.

David nodded. He realized that Loren often acted like a child. He remembered what one man in the community had said about Loren: "He never did learn to walk. He strutted from the day he was born."

"Pastor," Janice continued, "Loren can't keep a job. After a couple of weeks he tells everyone, including his employer, how things should be done. He's an expert on everything. I love him, but living with him is not easy."

She wiped her tears and continued, "We've had three kids in four years. I want to stay home with the girls, but we need my paycheck. We've borrowed money from my parents and we owe everyone. As our financial problems increase, so do the fights. We fight about his jobs and his leisure, including the time he spends hunting and fishing."

At David's encouragement Janice brought Loren to the next meeting. Upon arrival, he swaggered into the pastor's office and announced, "I'm here to help Janice with her problem." It went downhill from there. About the third session Janice said, "I feel like I'm raising the girls alone. You seldom go with me to school or to visit my folks. Every Sunday I have to pack up the kids by myself when I go to church."

Loren responded immediately. "The reason I don't go to church is simple," he nearly shouted. "I ain't baptized. I don't belong. I can't even take communion."

Loren soon grew tired of the meetings, but he knew he couldn't quit going unless something changed. It was unlikely that he would be able to get a better job immediately, and he sure wasn't about to give up hunting.

Then it struck him. He would get baptized. The simple act of Baptism would thrill Janice, please her parents, and put him in good with the pastor. It was perfect. All these benefits could be reaped for just a little effort. He made his announcement at the next counseling session. He was surprised when Pastor Zwanziger told him he had to participate in a class to prepare for Baptism, but at least the counseling sessions were over.

One day after work, Loren drove his car to Maynard Lennox's garage. Maynard, a quiet man with a perpetual smile, worked out of the garage next door to his home. For nearly three decades Maynard had allowed young men in the community to use his tools and equipment to do minor repairs.

At 6:00, Loren asked, "Mind if I come by tomorrow and finish this job?"

"You can stay right through the evening if you want," Maynard replied.

"I gotta run. Gotta meet with the minister at 7:00."

"You've been in church almost every Sunday lately," Maynard observed.

"What a man won't do to get some peace at home," Loren said. "Janice has been as ornery as a bear since the last baby was born. I figure an hour a week at church is a small price to pay for a truce."

"If you're going again tonight you're investing more than an hour," Maynard commented.

"I've got this all worked out," Loren boasted. "It's going to cost me six nights with the pastor to get baptized. It is no big deal and it makes a bunch of people feel good."

Suddenly Maynard's smile disappeared. "I'd be real careful about Baptism," he said slowly. "I wouldn't take Baptism lightly. It can change a fella—forever!"

Loren laughed nervously. "Good grief, man, what are you talking about? All I'm doing is going to have a little water sprinkled on my head and let the pastor say a few religious words. That don't amount to much."

Maynard's eyes narrowed. "Baptism isn't something you do. It is done to you. In Baptism, God makes you over. You are sealed with the Holy Spirit. I'm telling you, you are dealing with things that are not of this world. You'd better ask the pastor."

Later that evening, during his private class, Loren said, "Pastor, is there something dangerous about Baptism that you oughta tell us, or what?" David didn't understand what he meant, so Loren let the matter drop.

The next night when he returned to finish his work, Loren told Maynard what had happened.

"I don't understand ministers," Maynard said wiping the grease off his hands on an old rag. "Often they deal with powerful things of the Spirit as if nothing was going to happen. They serve communion like a bored waitress. They baptize with about as much enthusiasm as a five-year-old who was just told to take a bath. Listen, when the first Christians talked about Baptism they used words like *rebirth, drowning, crucifixion, cleansing*. They were talking about powerful stuff. The church expected that the person being baptized would be changed. "If anyone is in Christ they are a new creation," St. Paul said. Another time he wrote, "Don't you know that all of us who were baptized into Christ Jesus were baptized into his death?" Paul believed that the baptized person died. They were drowned before they were brought back to life. He said it was like death and resurrection. With their new life came a new name, which signified a new beginning."

Maynard walked over, picked up another rag, and kept wiping. "Through Baptism, lives get turned around. People are born anew. I'm one of them."

Loren seemed surprised. "I've known you for years. I've never thought of you as being all that religious."

"Now listen, I didn't say Baptism makes you more religious. I said it gives you new life. There's a difference." The mechanic paused for a few minutes as he remembered. "I was baptized by the Reverend Knute Lee when I was nineteen years old."

"My dad left home when I was six months and my mother moved in with my grandmother, who had two other daughters living at home," the mechanic continued. "I was twelve before I figured out the difference between an aunt, a grandmother, and a mother."

"At nineteen, I wanted out of the house and figured the quickest way was to get married. Before Barbara would marry me she wanted me to get baptized. So I went to visit Pastor Lee and asked him to 'do it' as soon as possible. He told me I wasn't ready. Told me that Baptism could alter my life and that I didn't have a clue. 'The rite of Baptism is very powerful,' he said. 'We don't know what wonders the Spirit is about to perform. A minister's only task is to conduct the service as correct as possible and to allow the Spirit to do God's work.' After a lot of conversations he baptized me, two weeks before the wedding."

Loren was puzzled. "So, when you were baptized, did your life change immediately?"

"No," Maynard said. "I stopped going to church as soon as we got married and never gave it another thought. I lived the way I had always lived. Barbara says I was both wild and self-centered. She says I was a rotten husband, and I suppose she's right. I know I wasn't much of a worker."

Maynard stopped occasionally to dig some dirt out of his fingernails. "Then, about a year after we got married, Goldie Olson died. She was the neighbor who spent more time with me than my own mother. The finest woman I had ever known. Sweet. Gentle. She had no kids, but I always figured she had more family than most of us. She acted as if we were all related. At the funeral, Knute said that Goldie's secret was that she had an identity. He put it something like this, 'Her Baptism told her who she was and whose she was.' For weeks after that funeral, I wondered if I'd ever know who I was."

The old mechanic paused as if he was trying to get all the facts straight. "Then one night a bunch of us were fooling around with water balloons. We were tired of throwing 'em at cars and began to toss 'em at each other. One of the guys fired a balloon at me and hit me square in the face. As the water dripped down he laughed, made a huge sign of the cross, and shouted, 'I just baptized ol' Maynard.'"

Maynard shook his head slowly as he remembered. "At first I laughed with everyone else. Then I thought, 'That sign of the cross is special to me.' I wondered if I had what Goldie had. Quickly I jumped into my car, drove over to Pastor Lee's house, and rang the bell. When he opened the door I said, 'I haven't thought about my Baptism since it happened. Is it still valid?'

"Pastor Lee stood there in his pajamas—it was about midnight— and said, 'Of course. God keeps his promises even when you don't. Besides, Baptism doesn't depend on you anyway. It is something that is done to you. Maynard, you are royalty, you are a child of the King. Go home.' And he closed the door."

The mechanic broke out in a big grin. "Child of the King. I couldn't have felt better if you had told me I just won the lottery. I had family. I wasn't a homeless, illegitimate child. I was claimed, signed, branded. I was royalty. I went home to tell Barbara. She was in bed. We talked a long time. Then we were gentle with each other. Somewhere about 3 A.M. she said, 'There is more you need to know. You're going to be a father. I'm three months pregnant.'

"I said, 'Why didn't you tell me this before?'

"She said, 'Because you have ignored me so much lately that I was thinking about moving away.'" Maynard just smiled and rubbed more grease off his hands.

Loren shook his head, saying, "That's a fine story, but why is Baptism dangerous?"

"It changed my life," Maynard said emphatically. "It changed my friends. Some old friends left me and I gained new brothers and sisters. I'm not complaining because I discovered I was a part of a family. I'm just saying to you, weigh the cost."

Loren protested, "Blazes, Maynard! I have a lot of buddies who are baptized, and they're just like me. I don't see no difference in their lives."

"Oh, it is possible even for royalty to live as if they were trash." Maynard agreed. "But at any minute the Spirit might start to work on a person and their life could change."

David concluded his story. "When Loren came to his next session, the last one before the Baptism, he talked without his usual bluster. At the end of the class he told me about his conversation with Maynard. It was clear that Maynard had taught him more about Baptism than I had."

Mary asked, "What about the Baptism itself?"

"Loren was frightened," David remembered. He could barely speak. He didn't even strut when he came forward to the font. Maynard was his sponsor.

Mary had listened to David carefully. "I've met Loren. I wouldn't exactly call him St. Francis."

David agreed. "Loren can still be abrasive and difficult. After all, Baptism doesn't provide a personality transplant. Besides, we all start at different places, but Loren did change. He now lives with a sense of thanksgiving and a need for forgiveness."

Mary persisted, "So you're convinced it is the work of the Spirit rather than the power of suggestion?"

"I don't pretend to understand everything that happens," David replied. "This much is sure, the Spirit used Maynard to help Loren and to help me. I now approach the sacraments expecting something to happen. I've learned that Baptism deals with death, birth, rebirth, drowning, and cleansing. I've learned that Christians are made, not born. I know that when I baptize I am dealing with things beyond my understanding. I know that God's goodness and grace are at work. That is why I tell people that Baptism may change their lives."

The Ball *of* Gold

This story was adapted from an Armenian folktale.

A rich couple and a poor couple lived next door to each other. The poor couple had a small child and were very happy. Sounds of laughter were frequently heard coming from their small home.

The rich couple had a larger home, but were never happy. No one heard sounds of joy coming from their house.

One day the rich woman said to her neighbor, "You are poor. Why is it that your home is a center of joy and ours is not? Nearly every night we can hear the sound of laughter spilling into the neighborhood from your house."

The poor woman, with a twinkle in her eye, said, "I guess it is our ball of gold. We constantly toss it back and forth. It gives us so much happiness."

The rich woman went home and told her husband, "The people next door who are always laughing have a gold ball that they toss back and forth all the time. Please, can we get a gold ball for our house?"

The next day the rich husband ordered a gold ball made. When he tried to throw it to his wife, however, it was so heavy that it hurt his wife's hands and crashed to the floor. Instead of happiness, once again they were both in tears.

The next morning the rich woman visited her neighbor. "You must tell me more about your gold ball," she said. My husband had one made and it hurt our hands and nearly ruined our house."

The poor woman was very apologetic. "When I spoke about a gold ball, I was referring to our wonderful child. We literally toss him back and forth, and he squeals with laughter. To us he is a ball of gold, and he fills our house with joy and love."

The Anniversary

*When Mike and Belinda got married they chose to do so
in front of the entire congregation during a Sunday morning
service. Their choice provided me an opportunity for a longer
than normal wedding sermon, and an occasion to speak
about several crucial marital issues, including sex,
to the entire congregation.*

Hans Nielsen Hauge Park was the scene of a joyous celebration.
More than 300 guests gathered to celebrate the forty-fifth anniversary
of Speed and Helen Hanson. Most people agree that the endurance of
this union is one of the marvels of the Blackhawk community.

He was nineteen and she was twenty when they got married. Opin-
ions varied in those days regarding Speed's future; some thought he'd
be a professional comedian while others figured he'd spend time in jail.
However, everyone agreed that he was one of the craziest and most
likable kids they had ever met. His accomplishments in high school
are still legends. One of his classmates describes Speed's tenure at
Blackhawk High as "an extended prank, interrupted by occasional
visits to the classroom."

During his junior year, Speed and a couple of buddies had taken a
Plymouth apart and then reassembled it on the second-floor auditorium of the high school on a Sunday. When people arrived at school
the next day, they found the car running and the car doors locked.
School officials had been forced to evacuate the second floor until they
could get rid of the fumes. It took mechanics three days to get
the Plymouth out of the building. Getting it in took Speed only a
few hours.

Old friends love to tell about the time Speed had painted the stand-pipe in a neighboring town orange and black, the colors of Blackhawk High, or of the cows and pigs that he had frequently released in the school. They shake their heads when they recount how Speed had managed to get a manure spreader in five successive school parades.

Helen, on the other hand, was as refined and studious as Speed was rough and raucous. She was homecoming queen, church choir soloist, and salutatorian of her class. She was also a woman with a fiery temper.

The first years of the marriage were stormy. In the words of Speed, "We had a few fights that ranked up there with Louis-Schmelling and Fraser-Ali."

Somewhere around their tenth anniversary, a change came over both of them. Most people would tell you, "Speed got religion." He still had a crazy streak, but now he limited his pranks to an occasional snowball throwing contest on main street or decorating the statues in town to look like ski bums or hippies. His humor was no longer angry. Instead, he was a warm, funny man beloved by the entire community. No one was surprised to see the huge crowd for their forty-fifth anniversary.

The picnic began with a potluck. After dessert the three Hanson children asked everyone to gather while the honored couple opened their gifts. The first, round-trip tickets to Norway, was from the children. Speed accepted the present saying, "I plan to trade these in on two tickets to Hawaii. Why should I act like a crazy Norskie, freezing my knuckles in Trondheim, when I can sit in the sun at Waikiki?"

People laughed. Speed could read the minutes from a church council meeting and have people rolling in the aisles. For twenty years he had given the opening devotions at Sunday school during his tenure as superintendent and for twenty years children grew up thinking religion was fun. Most of them were surprised when they got to confirmation and found Bible stories weren't as humorous as the version Speed told.

After each present was opened, Speed told stories about Helen and the kids. Mostly he made fun of himself. People were all having a wonderful time. Suddenly one of his friend's shouted, "Tell us about one of your donnybrooks with Helen."

Speed's reply was short and serious, "All of that is in the past."

Then Gladys Olson, president of the Women's Church Club, stood and said somberly, "I am glad so many young people are here today. They can learn the true meaning of marriage from this wonderful couple."

Speed is indeed a deeply religious man, but he thinks people like Gladys give God a bad name. Quick as a flash he replied, "If I were to teach a course on marriage, my first lesson would be on sex and forgiveness." Gladys Olson gasped. Several folks did a quick check to see if Helen was ready to die of mortification, but she was smiling as if to say, "Tell 'em, Speed."

"I'm going to tell you something about marriage. First thing is you always marry a stranger. Take Helen and me. We went together six years. I worked on her dad's farm three summers before we got married. I thought I knew her like the back of my hand. The first three months after the wedding at least three or four times a day I would say, 'Who is this woman?' She'll tell you the same thing. At nineteen we're strangers to ourselves, so we certainly are a stranger to our spouse. How do you take two strangers and bring them together? Sex!"

This time several people gasped.

"I'm serious. When the good Lord says that the two will become one, he isn't talking about a joint checking account. Listen carefully, the Lord says, 'one flesh.' Whenever a man lies with a woman something almost otherworldly takes place, something spiritual. The reason sex is special and ought to be limited to people who have made a lifelong commitment is that the results of sex are lifelong. It is also sacred. More forgiveness has taken place in our bed than in all the confessionals in this town." Then he laughed. "Course I've had a little more to forgive than most people."

Speed was just warming up. "Every wedding sermon ought to have something in it about sex. I guess that ain't possible because half the ministers don't know anything about it and the pious ol' prune faces in the congregation would think it is crude to talk about such things. If they are so religious how can they ignore the words, 'Don't refuse your spouse?' Scripture isn't talking about passing the applesauce you know."

Speed stepped over and gave Helen a big juicy kiss and she patted him on the cheek. "I said the second thing is forgiveness. To get to that I have to tell you about me and Helen fightin'. We had a couple of battles that would make a marine proud. The last big one was a dandy. It took place late at night in January with me yellin' in my underwear and Helen yellin' right back in her bathrobe. Well, in those days I did things in dramatic form. After I had my say, I put on my coat over my Fruit-of-the Looms, kicked on my slippers, and headed out the door. I did that a couple of times, and it worked real well. Helen would cry, 'Don't leave me, Speed,' and I'd stay out long enough so that I could get my way when I came back."

Speed winked at his daughter Marie as if to say, 'You've heard all this before.' Then he continued. "I slammed the door, only my coat wasn't quite out yet. It got caught. I was in near zero temperatures with half a coat. I fumbled for the keys and discovered that they were in the part of the coat that was locked on the other side of the door. I was furious. I yelled. I pounded on the door. Helen didn't budge. I slipped out of my coat, and nearly froze. Finally I looked up and Helen was sitting in the window, laughing. Roaring. Tears rolling down her cheeks. I got madder. But then I was so cold I started laughing. She sat on the inside laughing and I sat on the outside laughing. Finally she opened the door and I fell inside. She looked at me and said, 'Do you give up?' I said, 'I do.' Then all of a sudden we both laughed again. We had just renewed our vows, in the midst of a fight. She said to me, 'Come to bed and I'll warm you up.' And she did. Right there we forgave each other. And God, who had heard my 'I do,' pronounced us man and wife again. It was a moment when we experienced God's grace. God can use even our foolish pride in bringing us back together."

Speed stood still for a moment considering whether he ought to say more. Helen made the decision for him, jumping to her feet and addressing her friends. "As usual Speed didn't quite say enough," she began with a wink. "When he needed to say is that love is not the center of marriage. Commitment is. Love doesn't make the marriage possible. Marriage makes love possible. Our love is weak; at least my love is. I need something to support it. Marriage does that. Marriage helps me keep my promise. Isn't that what marriage is, a public promise? That's why infidelity is so serious. If you break your word, what do you have? It is also why we need God. God keeps his promises to us and in so doing helps us keep ours."

Helen walked over to a bench and threw her arms around a small man sitting with his arms crossed. "One of the ways that God helped us to keep our promises is my brother-in-law Tom, here. He has always been level-headed. From the day of our wedding, he has not merely been a friend of mine, he has been a friend of our marriage. More than once when times were tough, he would take Speed aside and say, 'You got a great wife, Speed.' Not long after that he would find me alone and say, 'You got a great husband, Helen.' If every marriage had a friend like Tom, there would be a lot less problems."

After Helen concluded her little speech, the folks gathered around to talk. Then Marie, their oldest daughter, yelled, "Everybody come to see Mom and Dad cut the cake." People looked around and couldn't find Speed.

Pastor Zwanziger said, "I think I saw him going up the hill with the kids."

Helen laughed. "He promised to play 'Cowboys' with the grand-children. Well, he missed cutting the cake at our wedding too. That day he snuck out to pull some stunt on the minister's car. Pastor, you better check your Ford before you go home. I'll cut the cake alone."

An old woman said, "Do you think he'll ever change?"

Helen shook her head. "I never tried to change Speed. I figure if you need to change a person in order to marry him, you better think twice. All I did is love him." She smiled privately. "No. I don't think he will ever change. At least I hope he doesn't. I'll say this: Life with Speed is never boring." She smiled and looked a her friends. "I'll bet some of you can't make that statement."

CHAPTER II

Lent
and
Easter

A Second Chance

This story was written for Ash Wednesday.

Larry Munson had that fresh-off-the-farm look when he left home to go to college. Tall and muscular with a smile as big as his father's back forty, Larry was admired and respected by students and faculty alike. His dad, Thor, often boasted, "Larry has never given me a sleepless night. He's as strong as an ox and as gentle as a kitten."

In his second year at college Larry began to hang around with a fraternity known for its noisy parties. At first he seldom participated in the group's wild antics; he just watched from a distance.

One Friday night, when the guys were drinking at a county park, a gang of townies crashed the party. They taunted the frat boys until a small scuffle broke out. When blood began to flow down the face of one of his friends, Larry came out of the shadows. In an awesome display of strength, he broke the nose of one boy, left a terrible gash in the face of another and smashed in the windows of two cars.

The police were called, and Larry was booked for assault and malicious destruction of property. The judge noted that Larry had not provoked the incident and that he was a first-time offender, but refused to condone his violence. After a stern warning the judge assigned him to substance abuse counseling and put him on probation. His parents were mortified. The family decided to tell no one about the incident, and since Larry lived nearly 140 miles from the college, they were certain it would be kept as their little secret.

When school was out in May, Larry returned home and got a job working in construction. In mid-June he began to date Monica Froiland, a blue-eyed beauty he had long worshiped from afar. Never in his wildest dreams had he thought that anyone as lovely as Monica would ever be interested in him.

At first Monica seemed reluctant to see him more than once a week, but before the summer was over they were together every night. They enjoyed doing simple things together, like lying on the grass in the backyard and finding star pictures in the sky. Mostly they talked. Larry told her everything about his life at home and school, everything except the events of that one horrible night. If Monica found out he had a record or that he was forced to go through substance abuse counseling, he knew their relationship would be over.

Even if she would accept it, he was certain that her father and mother would not. Peter Froiland, Monica's father, was a highly respected math teacher at the high school, the teacher Larry admired more than any other.

In August, for the first time in his life, Larry had trouble sleeping and frequently felt depressed. Lois Munson noticed the change in her son and suggested he talk to Pastor Blom. "You've always been close to him," she reminded the young man.

Larry wanted to talk to his pastor, but he was afraid that the pastor would be hurt and disappointed when he learned about his behavior. When he closed his eyes he could imagine Pastor Blom shaking his head and saying, "Why, Larry? Why?"

In the fall, Larry and Monica returned to their separate schools. Larry moved off campus and selected a new group of friends. He avoided his old crowd, didn't drink, and attended chapel every week. Most of the time he felt fine, except when he talked to Monica on the phone. Following their conversation he almost always felt depressed. This continued all fall.

The young couple could hardly wait for Christmas vacation, but when December 20 finally came Larry was very uncomfortable. Even though he felt closer to Monica than ever before, he realized that there was a terrible barrier between them. All during Christmas break, whenever he went to her house, he broke out in a sweat. It was a relief to go back to school.

On Ash Wednesday, a roommate invited Larry to attend the Episcopal church at 7:15 A.M. Perhaps it was because he was in a strange church with a strange liturgy, but Larry was touched by this special service. He nearly wept when the priest put ashes on his forehead and said, "You are dust and to dust you shall return."

Larry felt like dust. Like dirt. Though he had only caught snatches of the sermon that spoke of confession, he became visibly shaken when the words of the Communion were spoken, ". . . given and shed for you for the forgiveness of sin." As Larry left the building in silence, he knew he was living a lie and he had to do something about it.

That evening Monica called to tell him she was coming for the weekend. "I'll be there Friday noon. I'm riding with my cousin Eric and I've called Ann, who says I can stay with her at the dorm."

From the moment Monica arrived she could tell that Larry was more troubled than ever before. Moments after they found a place to be alone he said, "I don't even know where to begin . . ." and then words came rushing out like a torrent. He blurted out the entire story, how he had lost control of himself, how he had hurt the other boys and smashed the car.

"Everyone was frightened of me," he sobbed, "and I was frightened of myself. I lost control. I'm ashamed of everything I did. I'm ashamed that I have deceived you and I don't blame you if you never want to see me again."

Monica took his hand. "I love you," she said simply. "I have known about your misadventures since we started dating." Larry stared at her in disbelief. "Dad told me," she continued. "He warned me that you were probably having a tough summer. At first I was shocked. I told Dad that I could never trust a man who had a violent temper."

Monica paused to wipe the tears that flowed down Larry's cheeks. "The day after Dad first told me he asked me to take a walk with him. Along the way he told me about two incidents that happened early in his life, before he met Mother. He said that he had shared these stories with Mother, but that he had never said anything about his shaded past to any of the three children. He said he guessed now was as good a time as any to tell me. He said, 'Monica, everyone deserves a second chance. What Larry did was stupid, not evil.' I asked Dad if I should raise the issue with you and he told me that it was important that you did it yourself. The last time we talked about this was at Christmas when Dad said, 'Is Larry still carrying that big weight on his back? I hope he'll give it up so he can start walking straight again.'"

The two sat together holding hands. After a long silence Monica said, "I have memorized a lot of scriptures about forgiveness. Would you like to hear some?"

Larry managed a smile while dabbing his eyes. "I never dreamed we'd end up sharing Bible verses together, but I'm ready for anything."

"If we confess our sins, God is faithful and just and will forgive us our sins and cleanse us from all unrighteousness."

Larry nodded. "I ought to know that one. It's a part of the confession each Sunday morning."

Monica smiled again. "Whoever is in Christ is a new creature. The old has passed away, behold the new has come."

Larry said, "Do you really believe that we can become new?"

Monica said, "I believe that when you have the sins of the past forgiven, and eliminated, that every day can be a new day. It is like Dad said, without forgiveness we carry a ten-pound weight." She paused and looked at Larry's massive body. "In your case it is probably a fifty-pound weight."

Larry said, "I guess Lent is about as good a time as any to start over. Pastor Blom used to call Lent a time for spring cleaning. I guess he meant that if you confess your sins, God can sweep them out."

"And, if you confess them, no one can hold them over you again. You are free."

Larry frowned. "I'm going to have to have a talk with your folks."

"How about adding Pastor Blom to the list?"

"Absolutely not," Larry said emphatically. "He'll be heartbroken. He'll never respect me again."

Monica said quietly, "He knows."

Larry was astonished. "He never treated me any different!"

Monica's eyes flashed. "Why does everyone think Christians are surprised at sin? He understands, because, like my dad, he's also a sinner. My hunch is the only one left to forgive Larry, is Larry."

Two Funerals

On a Friday in Lent, a card arrived in the mail that caught David Zwanziger's attention. "God never places more on us than we can handle," the card read. David taped it just above his desk.

Ten days earlier, Howard Iverson, David's friend, neighbor, and parishioner, died. Howard and his wife Elsie had retired from farming about the time the Zwanzigers arrived in Blackhawk. The Zwanziger children quickly had adopted the Iversons, calling them "Gramps" and "Grams." David and his wife, Doris, had also struck up a friendship with the Iverson's only child, Iris, and her husband, Don.

The funeral service, held on a Thursday, was simple. It began with three of Howard's favorite Bible passages, which he had preselected years ago. Next was a sermon, a prayer written by Iris, and "Precious Lord, Take My Hand," sung by a quartet.

Elsie sat passively through the entire service, displaying no emotion over the death of her husband of forty-three years.

After the benediction, the pall bearers began to wheel the draped casket down the aisle. Iris followed, with her mother on her arm. Suddenly Elsie collapsed. Someone screamed. A nurse in attendance pushed her way to Elsie's side through the frightened congregation. David sprinted to his office to call the rescue squad. People stood by in stunned silence as the EMS squad rushed into the church, carefully lifted Elsie onto a cart and wheeled her to a waiting vehicle. People followed the cart outside and watched as the ambulance, siren crying, sped to its destination four blocks away.

It seemed but a few minutes when the phone call from the hospital confirmed what everyone feared. Elsie had died instantly.

David, who had followed the ambulance to the hospital, came back to the church where a handful of people were eating potato salad and meat sandwiches in the church basement. Unable to talk, he went to his office and stared at the walls. Later in the day he found himself at the Iverson home with Iris and Don. As he sat he tried in vain to think of something to say—a word of comfort, a word of hope. Everything he thought of seemed trivial. He didn't even invite the family to pray fearing he would be speechless. Finally he broke the silence. "When do you plan to have your mother's funeral?" David asked.

"As soon as possible. Saturday, if that is okay with you," Iris replied. "Everyone who is coming is already in town."

The Saturday service was by far the most difficult funeral David had ever conducted. When he stepped to the pulpit to speak, he sensed the congregation was recording his every word. People were hoping the pastor would help make sense of the situation. David, however, felt hollow, and he was certain his words sounded empty.

On Monday, his normal day off, David made the visits he had neglected the previous week. First he stopped at the retirement center, the Ebenezer Home. Normally David enjoyed joking with the aides, playing euchre with a couple of men, and praying with others. On this day he found Ebenezer depressing.

It was worse when he visited the hospital. He nearly choked when he walked down the corridor. What was that smell? One of the patients was a small boy who had leukemia. David greeted the mother, spoke briefly with the boy, said a prayer, and left. As he walked out of the hospital he felt like Robo-Pastor. It had not been a very engaging visit.

That night after the children left the supper table, David's wife, Doris, asked, "What's wrong?"

"I'm sick of Wisconsin winters; I'm sick of Lent; and I'm tired of my job," David said. "I'm ready for Easter."

Fifteen minutes later the phone rang. It was Knute Lee, a retired pastor who reminded David of a marine sergeant. Knute usually omitted greetings or salutations. "David, you normally study next Sunday's text on Tuesday mornings. Do you plan to do so tomorrow?"

David hadn't even thought about it. "I guess so," he muttered.

"Then I will be at your office at 9 A.M. We'll read and study together." Before he could respond, Knute hung up. David wasn't sure he wanted anyone in his office in the morning, but there was no denying Knute, one of the most persistent men he had ever met.

When David arrived at church the next morning, Knute was in the kitchen brewing a pot of coffee. The two pastors were about to begin when Iris walked in unexpectedly. David started to tell Knute that they would postpone their study when the older pastor spoke. "Iris, we are about to study the gospel for the next Sunday, the Fifth Sunday in Lent. Would you like to join us?"

David was surprised when Iris eagerly accepted the invitation and sat down. Knute offered a prayer and asked Iris to read the story of Jesus and Lazarus.

Iris had read but a few verses when David began to feel ill. The longer Iris read, the worse David felt. By the time the reading was completed, he told his companions he was unable to continue.

"Do you think you have the flu?" Iris asked kindly.

"I don't know what it is," David confessed. "I've had something for several days."

"What strikes you about this story?" Knute asked, ignoring the state of David's health.

A flash of irritation swept over David. He felt like saying, "Knute, will you listen? I'm not feeling well." Instead, he answered the question. "It isn't the most significant thing in the story, but I am struck by the first words of both sisters. Jesus walks miles to get to the place and immediately they try to lay a guilt trip on him. 'If you would have been here my brother would not have died.' I hear things like that a lot."

"It is not a very cheery story, is it?" Iris said.

David agreed. "A man gets ill; Jesus, for some strange reason, takes his time leaving. The man dies. His disciples are afraid they are going to get killed. Martha criticizes him once he arrives, and it ends with the high priest plotting his death. It is enough to make you sick."

Knute nodded. "And it did."

"I don't think the way I feel has anything to do with the story," David protested.

Knute leaned forward, and spoke gently, "How do you evaluate your part in the two Iverson funerals?"

Tears immediately filled David's eyes. "On a scale of one to ten, I was a minus two. I'm afraid I wasn't a very good pastor. I was too shocked to be of much help to Iris and Don on Thursday and I was almost disoriented at Elsie's funeral. I'd say it was pretty pitiful." He turned to Iris, "I'm sorry I was of so little help."

Iris looked surprised. "I didn't see it that way at all. Don and I weren't looking for any great words of wisdom the night Mom died. We were just glad you were there. You reacted like Jesus did when he saw the grief of the family. He wept. I am very grateful that you have been with us during these difficult times. The reason I came by this morning was to thank you. You helped me understand that I was not the only one who had experienced grief. I lost my parents, but you lost dear friends. Everything you did told me that you loved them dearly. That was very important to me."

"I couldn't even pray with you," David said choking back the tears.

"I found the entire visit a prayer. It was enough just to have you with us. I told Don this morning that I have felt the presence of God more powerfully in the last week than ever before in my life. He said something that baffled me at first, 'Faith sees best in the dark.' The more I think about it, the more I like it. What does that say to you?"

Knute broke in. "The first thing it says is that your husband is a perceptive person and a fine theologian. More people lose faith during good times than in bad times. Bright lights make us think we can find our own way. In the darkness we know we need the light."

Iris picked up the Bible. "Mind if I respond to Knute's question? I am struck by the presence of death everywhere in this story. Perhaps it is because I've been thinking about death a lot lately, but I can even smell it. Martha says, 'Lord, already there is a stench because he has been dead four days.' It just seems to me that the odor is everywhere. Every day there is a story in the newspaper about a child, a teen, or a young adult who died in a tragic way. Some are killed in accidents while others inject death into their bodies through drugs, steroids or alcohol. The money we so desperately need for life—for the care of the very young, the very old, and the very poor, for health care— is invested in weapons of death. The stench of death is everywhere."

Knute asked, "And do you see any hope?"

Iris nodded. "I am the Resurrection and the Life. That is the hope. The hope isn't in humans, it is in God. God can bring life in the midst of death. God weeps over the death of his creation, just as Jesus wept, and just as David wept. Of course there is this one important distinction, God is not willing to let death be the last word. Howard and Elsie are in the hands of God. That is a very great comfort."

It was Knute's turn. "The world uses death as a tool. Like the high priest says, it is a matter of expediency. He figures that it is no big deal that one person die so that the rest of the nation need not suffer. Governments are willing to lose a few for the sake of a military action. They use death as a threat—ask the Croats, the Serbs, or the Kurds.

"God uses death too, but not as a threat. He uses the death of Jesus to give life. He uses his own death in order to give hope and 'to gather into one the dispersed children of God.'"

David had listened intently to the exchange of the two friends. "Iris is right. Death is all around us. I started to feel nauseated when Elsie died. Since that time I have smelled death wherever I went. When he read the story, it became overpowering. By the way, I'm feeling better."

Tears again filled David's eyes. "I'm afraid I have had a few things backwards. I have tried to be the resurrection and the life. It was not enough to tell of the one who is resurrection. I had to have answers and I had to be strong. When I had no answers and no strength, I felt like people were blaming me, just as Martha blamed Jesus. But Don and Iris don't need me to be their comfort. The one who is the resurrection and the life is comfort enough."

Knute nodded. "Even pastors need to hear God's good news. Let me offer one more image from this story. I am struck by Lazarus coming forth from the grave, with the burial cloths wrapped around him. He had just been resurrected, but the signs of death were still evident. I see this as a parable of our time. We live by the grace and power of God, but death is still very much present. We live as Easter people in a Good Friday world. Jesus is the resurrection and the life, but we still live in a world of pain. Sickness, disease, anger, hatred, war—these are but a few of the burial cloths wrapped around us."

Knute let his words sink in before he concluded. "Jesus issues a command, 'Unbind him, and let him go.' We all need to be unbound. David needed God to unbind him from his need to play God, because that is certainly death. Others need to be unbound from hatred or envy or greed. The more deeply we enter into his life, the more deeply we need to experience resurrection."

They finished their study at about 10:30. At 12:45 David came home for lunch. Doris asked, "What did you do this morning?"

David laughed. "I got sick. And I got better. Seriously, after our study I went to the hospital to visit the little boy with leukemia. Then I made a visit at Ebenezer."

"I thought you just made those visits yesterday," she said.

"No, that was Robo-Pastor. Today I visited after a few bandages were unwrapped. It is amazing what you see when you become unbound. It was wonderful. And you know what? It even smelled different today.

The Noon Bible Study

The people of Blackhawk, Wisconsin, though not opposed to controversy, are not really accustomed to it. With only one school, one major restaurant (Little Oslo), and one theater in this town of 3,000, there is very little to debate. People don't even argue about religion since eight of the twelve churches with a Blackhawk address are Norwegian Lutheran.

At First Lutheran, the largest of the two Lutheran churches in the Blackhawk city limits, Harold Hauge, a quiet cautious man, has managed to avoid all open conflict during the eighteen years that he has served as pastor. Harold is known as "The Great Peacemaker" to his friends.

David Zwanziger, the pastor at "the other Lutheran church," officially known as Maple Street Lutheran, is a man of much different spirit. He is as bold as Harold is cautious. Since the day of his arrival three years ago, fresh from seminary, he has challenged the old ways. His mere presence challenged a time-honored tradition of Norwegian pastoral leadership and raised one significant question among many Blackhawk residents: "How did a German with the name of Zwanziger end up in our community?" Some people believe it a part of the Lutheran Church's affirmative action program.

About six months ago David talked Harold into co-leading a Men's Bible Study once a week. His proposal was to study the lessons for the following Sunday. When they couldn't agree which church ought to be host, Moose Davis invited them to meet in the back room of his restaurant, Little Oslo, each Thursday.

At first the idea of a joint Men's Bible Study seemed strange because everyone knew the two pastors were as different as fire and ice. The group started small, but what appeared as a disadvantage soon started attracting crowds. Though it was painful for him, Harold Hauge felt forced to take issue with a number of David's crazy new ideas. The two pastors disagreed so often that people started coming in big numbers just to listen to the arguments. Before long, women also started coming, forcing the churches to officially change the name to the Noon Bible Study. Unofficially everyone, including the women, still call it "Men's Bible Study."

One Thursday the study focused on Luke 17:1-10, the gospel for the next Sunday. When both pastors finished their opening remarks, Trygvie Lien stood up to speak. Trygvie is a retired art teacher and is regarded by most people as an agnostic, or even worse, a liberal. Nearly everyone thinks Trygvie has read too much "new thinking."

"You know," Trygvie began, "every week we talk about all these ideas in the Bible, but no one dares to connect them to what is going on right here in Blackhawk. We keep everything vague and abstract. We ought to talk about specific events here at home."

Harold Hauge nervously replied, "I don't think it is appropriate to embarrass people or point fingers at folks. That is not our purpose."

Before Trygvie could sit down, David Zwanziger, who sensed a great opportunity, interrupted, "What do you have in mind, Trygvie? Do you see a connection here?"

The whole room held its breath as Trygvie cleared his throat. "As a matter of fact I do. I'm looking at this passage that says, 'If your brother sins, rebuke him and if he repents, forgive him. If he sins against you seven times in one day, and each time he comes to you saying, 'I repent,' you must forgive him.'"

He paused, looked around the room and said, "I think this passage is about Todd Ostrem." The whole room gasped.

Not long ago Todd had been caught in a tax evasion scheme and had lost his job. Since that time he'd been without work. "Everybody knows that Todd was guilty," Trygvie continued. "He has said as much, but nobody forgives him."

One of the businessmen said, "I don't think that is fair. I don't hold it against him. I forgive him."

Trygvie snapped, "Then why don't you offer Todd a job? The way you really forgive a person is to let them start over. You give them another chance. There are a lot of you here who need a good worker, but nobody has offered him a second opportunity."

As Harold Hauge squirmed nervously in his chair, David Zwanziger leaned forward, a smile on his face. Then he recognized a person toward the back of the room whose hand was part way up. It was Mildred Thompson.

Now, it was almost an unwritten rule that though the women could attend, they didn't talk. Mildred was hesitant, but when Pastor David called on her she took courage.

"When you first read that part about how terrible it will be for those who make others sin, or causes the little ones to sin, I was thinking about some of the children at the high school," Mildred said softly. "I was thinking about people who buy beer or supply drugs to them. I assume that is one valid interpretation, isn't it?"

David responded, "I sure think that getting kids hooked on drugs is leading them astray. You're suggesting that older children who sell them booze or something are causing little ones to sin?"

"Well," Mildred answered slowly, "that is what I thought initially, but the more I reflect I think the real problem is with me and my friends, adults who can't seem to have a gathering, a party, or a get-together without some kind of alcohol present. Perhaps we are the ones who lead children astray by suggesting, by example, that people can't have a good time without alcohol."

The room buzzed with disapproval. It is one thing to criticize kids, but quite another to point the finger at adults. As the whispers continued, David spoke directly to Mildred who had sat down. "That was a very courageous thing to say."

Mildred bounced to her feet again. "As long as I'm at it," she said looking around the room, "I have one more idea. You all know that Clarence and I operated our camera shop for nearly twenty years, until he got sick three years ago. What struck me when Trygvie got to talking was that someone must of taught Todd how to change those books around. I admit I've always liked him. He used to come in the shop a lot and talk photography with Clarence. But who put those ideas in his head? If we cheat on our taxes, if we take a little money out of our cash register without reporting it, if we condone little forms of dishonesty, if we say, 'everyone does it,' aren't we encouraging people to sin? Maybe when the Lord says 'little ones' he doesn't mean children, maybe he means ones that are easily led astray. If that's true, a lot of us need to do some confessing."

Roger Trygestad, a farmer, who many think is a frustrated preacher, frequently stands up and gives a little sermon. Holding his Bible in the air like Billy Graham, he usually says something like, "If we only had a bit more faith, if we all just believed more, everything would be okay." Most people also think that this is basically the same message Harold Hauge preaches, but that Roger is a better public speaker. Last Thursday he was true to form. He jumped to his feet and held forth about the importance of faith. As he spoke he waved his Bible above his head, swinging it back and forth like it was made of rubber. This time he hadn't gone very far when the young pastor interrupted.

"Roger, I think you are missing the point of this story." The farmer swung around and for a moment his fierce gray eyes blazed at the minister. "Read verses five and six of the seventeenth chapter of Luke," David continued. "After the disciples listen to what Jesus says they get all worked up and say, 'Make our faith greater.' Jesus then told them that even a little bit of faith can work wonders. Even faith as small as a mustard seed can tear up trees. The disciples were using their lack of faith as an excuse for not following Jesus and he says, 'You have plenty of faith, you just aren't acting on it. It isn't a matter of not having enough faith, it is a matter of doing something with what you have.'"

Roger was about to launch into a counterattack when Moose Davis said that if anyone wanted dessert they should pass their plates down to the end of the table. Pastor Hauge, already shaken over all the controversy, used this as an opportunity to quiet things down. He spoke, without taking a breath, saying things like, "Everyone sure has had a lot to think about" and "There is still one more part to the text that talks about servants doing their jobs and then not getting a lot of thanks for it." He then reminded everyone that they were all just to say, "We are ordinary servants; we have only done our duty." He explained that the apple pie they were about to eat had come from Selmer Torgerson's orchard and that Bernice had made it fresh that morning, and that normally she was embarrassed whenever anyone said she was a great cook. "Maybe," he concluded, "Bernice is like those that see cooking and helping as what they ought to do and don't expect thanks." Then he asked everyone to bow their heads, and he closed with prayer before another argument broke out.

By the following Tuesday, Todd had already received a couple of job offers. He planned to take two days to think it over.

The following Thursday, Moose had to set up three more tables. People who came for the first time said they were told by friends that the "Noon Bible Study," was the best show in town.

The Lottery

While growing up, Eric Hauge and Gary Tollickson were inseparable. Blessed with charming smiles and playful spirits, the two lads were natural leaders. When they were nine they began to play a game in the woods on the southwest side of town. It was something like cowboys and Indians, or maybe settlers and Indians. Eric, the scout in these games, took the name "Hawk." Gary, the wagon master, became "Kit," as in Kit Carson.

Though the games didn't last, the names and friendship did. They played on the same basketball and baseball teams, double dated, sang in the same choir, and attended the same church. The boys did have their differences. Kit was more quiet and studious. Hawk, a born clown, was generally the life of the party. With his hat turned sideways and his quick one-liners, he could laugh at himself or gently tease others, even people who seemed very serious.

After graduation both young men enrolled at the same college. Hawk lasted a semester, deciding he wasn't made for "book work." He got a job at Heavenly Holstein Creamery at age nineteen, and married Rita, his first girlfriend. When Kit finished school he came back home to open "Tollickson's Accounting Services." At twenty-two, he married Marlene, Rita's best friend and the first girl he ever dated. The two men were as inseparable as adults as they had been as children. They frequently hunted and fished together. Seldom a week passed when the families—Hawk, Rita, and their three girls, and Kit, Marlene, and their two boys—didn't get together. Both couples were active in church, serving in leadership positions.

Eight years after he first went to work for Heavenly Holstein, Hawk had become a certified cheesemaker. It was steady work, and when they added Rita's salary from her part-time job as a secretary at the board of education, they made ends meet. They lived simple lives. Each day Hawk rode an old bike to work and back. Few people saw him ride in the morning because his day began at 5 A.M. By contrast, nearly everyone in town had witnessed his return home at one time or another. The trip was pure show biz. Either he rode backwards, sitting on his handlebars, or, he rode with one foot on the seat. People always waved to him, and Hawk, dressed in the white shirt and pants of a cheesemaker, waved back.

One Saturday night in August, when the two families were eating pizza at the Tollickson home and preparing for their euchre game, an announcement came over Channel 8 that changed Hawk's life. The winning number from the state lottery rolled across the bottom of the screen. Hawk had played the same numbers for years, a combination of his street address, high school basketball jersey, and birth date. The number on the screen was his number. He went crazy. The whole house went crazy. By the following week when Hawk went to Madison to accept his check for $146,396—the first of twenty annual payments, the whole town went crazy.

It is hard to follow the sequence of events after that night in August. About two weeks later he and Rita rented the Mississippi Queen, the pride of the great river, to take about forty friends for a celebration ride. Hawk's only instruction to the captain was, "Go slow! I want this party to last."

The following week Hawk rented a sound truck to play "Take This Job and Shove It!" in front of the Heavenly Holstein. He decided to quit work in style.

Next, he ditched the bike that had made him famous and bought a new red convertible. When it arrived he vowed, "The top will never be up until the day I get rid of it." August was just one long party.

When Rita went back to work the first of September, Hawk was a free man. He had met new friends who went to stock car races with him on Tuesdays, and high school football games on Fridays. They also took frequent hunting trips together. Though it was only a two-hour drive to Madison to see the Badgers play Saturday football, it was noon on Sunday before he got back. Sometimes Rita went with him, but often he went without her.

In late fall, hunting took up most of his time. The fourteen-day deer season lasted over four weeks for Hawk. It took over a week to open camp and six days to close it. In January he began ice fishing. In the spring he traveled all over the state to the best trout steams. The first of May he bought a new Harley Davidson.

When he was home he often stayed up late recording movies on one of his VCRs, or transferring music from his new compact-disc player to audio cassette.

As the days passed he seldom saw Kit. "It's strange," Hawk thought. "My old pal must be jealous of my good fortune." He missed Kit, but life was going so fast he really didn't have time to think about it.

Over the Fourth of July, Hawk went north to Hayward with a bunch of new buddies to fish for muskies. Rita wasn't very happy about his being gone again, particularly over a holiday. The argument that began in private continued in front of his friends while he was loading the car. Later he told the guys, "She's been getting her nose in a twit a lot lately. She'll get over it."

The July 4th argument continued for weeks. They were still, in his words, "exchanging ideas," the last Friday in July when he and another group of friends left for Milwaukee to catch a three-game series between the Brewers and the Yankees. When he got home late Sunday night the house was empty. He found a note pinned to his pillow: "I can't stand this life anymore. I need time to think. Rita."

At first he was angry. He threw the pillows and kicked the bed, almost breaking his big toe. He filled the air with some choice remarks. Suspecting his wife and children were with her parents, he first tried their home about 2 A.M. No one answered. That left the cottage, which had no phone. He called the Tollicksons. A sleepy Marlene answered. When he asked, "Where's Rita?" her answer was evasive. Hawk exploded, "I have every right to know where my wife and kids are!"

Now fully awake, Marlene's voice was calm and clear. "Rita needed to get away. I'm sure she will be in touch with you soon. I'm sorry, Hawk. Good night."

The next day Hawk made a couple of calls, confirming what he suspected: Rita and the girls were at her parents' cottage, about three hours north. What he also found out was that Marlene and Kit had driven them up on Friday. He felt angry and betrayed by his oldest friend, a friend he hadn't talked to in three months. It was time for that talk.

Hawk parked the convertible outside of Kit's accounting business, located beneath First National Bank. Hawk never touched the bottom four steps as he stormed through the front door and demanded, "Is Benedict Arnold in his office?"

The secretary didn't have to answer. The door to Kit's office opened immediately and the old friend spoke, "I was hoping you'd stop by. Come on in."

Hawk was shouting before the door closed, "Where do you get off tearing my wife and family away from me?" The volume was several decibels above the roar of a 747.

Kit's voice was calm. "Rita thinks you are the one who has done the separating. She thinks you've been everywhere but home for months. She isn't even sure she's married to the same guy. I think she's right."

"A fine friend you've been," Hawk shouted. "When I really need you, you take the side of Rita."

"Hawk, you haven't needed me in months. You cut yourself off from Marlene and me shortly after you struck it rich."

"I cut myself off from you? I can't believe my ears. You became jealous of my success. You couldn't stand to see me make it big. Kit, you abandoned me."

Kit sat down next to his old friend. "Hawk, that isn't true. Marlene and I rejoiced for you. At first we even tried to keep up with you. We loved the trip down the Mississippi, but soon you were more concerned with your toys and gadgets than your old friends. We stopped seeing you when you wanted to go everywhere without the kids. Hawk, you've been a stranger to those girls for months."

Hawk was desperate. "I thought you would understand. I thought you knew what a break I had. It freed me from that danged job. It made it possible for me to be somebody. I was tired of going without the things most people had. I was tired of working fifty hours a week and just barely getting by. I was tired of having to save eleven months for a lousy two week vacation." Hawk began to cry.

Kit reached over and took his old buddy by the arm. "Hawk, I'm not trying to romanticize your life, but the way you lived and worked was both honest and honorable. You were a good cheesemaker. You were a good husband and a good father. You have a great wife and fine kids. You're healthy."

Hawk looked up, his eyes pleading. "But Kit, isn't there more to life than all this? I was hungry for something more."

"Of course you were. But did your new convertible satisfy you? Did that new Harley Davidson take care of your hunger, or that snow-mobile, or the two fancy VCRs?"

Hawk laughed through his tears. "If you're going to bawl me out, at least get the facts straight. There are *three* fancy VCRs."

Kit got serious. "A man's life does not consist in the abundance of his possessions."

"Is this the start of a sermon?"

"If my oldest friend needs a sermon, I'm willing to try preaching. Your good fortune provided you with extra money and time. You chose to invest your new income in trinkets and appliances. You have invested your newfound leisure in activities that separate you from the children who adore you and the wife who loves you. When you were making cheese you had time to coach softball. Now you seldom have time to watch your girls play. Do you really think you and your family is better off today than you were before the lottery? Do all these new gadgets really satisfy you?"

"Three days ago I would have shouted yes to both questions! I would have told you I was having the time of my life. I was traveling so fast I didn't even see where I was going." Hawk thought for a moment. "Kit, do you remember our games in the woods on hot days? I used to take a canteen along. After we scouted the territory we used to swig grape Kool-Aid together. Remember how the more we drank the thirstier we became? I guess the last eleven and one-half months have been like drinking Kool-Aid."

Hawk paused, wiped his eyes, and said, "So how do I satisfy my hunger, my thirst? Will Rita come back?"

Kit leaned forward. "I'll answer the second question, and we'll both answer the first. Rita loves you and wants to come back, but I don't think she is interested in the destructive you. She needs assurances that you want her. The girls want their daddy. And as for the first question, you know the answer to that one as well as I do. You don't satisfy your hunger with that which rusts, corrodes, or wears out. Rather than putting things at the center of your life, you need to put a person. That person is Jesus Christ. That is why the Bible calls Jesus the Bread of Life. Hawk, you know that as well as I do."

"Kit, you know I haven't stopped going to church in the last year."

"No, but you've stopped listening. Your ears have been plugged. You've allowed money to become a curse, rather than a blessing. You've forgotten that all of our gifts are from God and are intended to benefit the whole community. Somewhere Jesus suggests that it is more difficult for the rich to enter the kingdom of God than the poor. You need more time to pray. You need to listen even more carefully to Christ in order to learn how to handle your seductive newfound wealth. I believe yours is a spiritual problem, Hawk."

The two old friends talked for another half hour. Just before a rather somber Hawk went home, the two men embraced.

On Wednesday, Hawk drove up to the cottage to see Rita and the kids. They knew something was different when he drove in with the top up on the convertible and a sign in the window that said, "FOR SALE." When he arrived he said, "I'm only up for the day. I know you need more time to think."

The following Sunday, he went to church with Kit and Marlene. The gospel, from the sixth chapter of John, included these words, "Do not work for the food that spoils, but for the food which endures to eternal life, which the Son of man will give you."

When the service was finished, Hawk evaluated the sermon with his best friend before they left the church, "First of all, they've got the wrong guy preaching. On the subject of perishable food, I'm the head chef. Second, the pastor needed to put it more forcefully. When we invest all of our efforts on things that don't last, we are wasting precious gifts. The only life that makes any sense is one where we invest in people and God."

After he finished with his analysis of the spoken Word, Hawk walked Kit and Marlene to their car. "Rita and the kids are coming home on Friday," he said. "Will you join us for pizza on Saturday?"

Kit grinned, "We'd love to."

"By the way," Hawk said turning to Marlene, "I'm probably going back to work in a week or so. I'm close to working out a deal at Heavenly Holstein." Marlene gasped, "You're going back to making cheese?"

"Not exactly. The two owners were looking for another partner and I was looking for an investment. Besides, owners have more time to coach softball than cheesemakers. Right now things are in the hands of my accountant."

Marlene looked at Kit, "You knew about this and didn't tell me, right?"

Kit smiled, "At Tollickson Accounting Services, confidentiality is a part of the contract."

Marlene frowned. "You said you are close. What is holding up the deal?"

"Perks," Hawk said with a sly grin. "I'm negotiating a canopied parking spot for my bike."

Family Feud

When Pastor David Zwanziger arrived at his first parish several years ago, he discovered the little town had a fascination for nicknames. He learned that druggist O. R. Paulson is called "Wolf" because when he was a boy he called the police to report that a wolf was loose in the neighborhood. It turned out to be a large cat, but the name stuck. Elmer Dregne, who owns the local body shop, is known as "Crash," Reid Ellefson, the town's fire chief is nicknamed "Blaze," and everyone calls Wayne Monson, a 6-foot-6-inch giant who runs a fix-it business, "Tinker."

Sometimes entire families, such as the Bolstads, have interesting names. August Bolstad was chair of the committee that brought David to town. He had the reputation of being a fine biblical scholar. August had attended numerous lay institutes of theology and had even taken Greek in order to read biblical commentaries. David thought nothing of August's name until he met the three Bolstad sisters, all members of the church. Their names—April, May, and June. Surely, David thought, this must be a family with a great sense of humor. In fact, the four Bolstads had seemed to be a jolly group, until about three years ago when their mother Tillie died. The events surrounding Tillie Bolstad's death had caused a painful split in the household.

The sibling squabble broke out over the disposition of Tillie's property. It was, as one local wit said, spring against summer. April and May were on one side, June and August on the other.

During his first visit to the house after his mother died, August found messages under three antique lamps and on the backside of several pictures. The messages read, "This is for April," or "This is for May."

All four children had long believed that Tillie never completed a will. When they opened their mother's safety deposit box, however, they discovered that she left a detailed will which included a list of what every child was to receive, down to the silverware. Her list and the names on the backs of the lamps and pictures did not match. It was pretty clear to June and August that the messages were written not by their mother, but by their sisters. World War III broke out in the Bolstad family.

In the weeks that followed, each pair threatened the other with a lawsuit. Hardly a day passed when some juicy tidbit wasn't released into the town's gossip mill. One week people were buzzing over what August did to April, and the next week over what May did to June.

David, as the pastor of the Fighting Bolstads, preferred not to get involved in this family feud, yet found it increasingly difficult to avoid it. All four Bolstads attended church every Sunday, and April and August never missed the Sunday morning Bible class. Neither was willing to let the other prevent them from attending, but the minute they arrived their icy stares seemed to make the temperature in the room drop. The family feud made everyone in the church uncomfortable.

Finally David decided something should be done. But what? Should he visit each of them separately? Should he call them all together? Then one day, as he was working on his upcoming sermons, he discovered that two of the lessons seemed to directly address the issue facing the family. David quickly developed a strategy.

During the following Sunday's Bible class, the pastor announced that next month they would postpone their study of the Prophets and focus on the gospel for the next week. He said, "I'm going to ask some of you to do a little homework for that class. I'll call you this week."

The first week the group studied Matthew 18:15-20. "In this passage Jesus gives us instructions on how to deal with grievances between believers," David said. "I'll read just a section. 'If your brother or sister sins against you, go to them and show them their fault. Do it privately. If they listen you have won your brother or sister back.'"

Although there was a lot of discussion, neither August nor April, normally quite vocal, took part. In conclusion David said, "The purpose of these instructions is to help us win back those we love. It grows out of a conviction that we are to forgive the way we are forgiven."

The following week David made separate phone calls to April and August to ask them to write a brief paragraph for next Sunday's class. After hesitating, each agreed. Unknown to the other, David gave them both the same assignment. "I'd like you to write 50 to 100 words on the "unforgivable sin," he said.

The next Sunday David announced the topic and said, "I've asked two people to prepare something to get the discussion started." He then called on April.

"The concept of the unforgivable sin rests on Jesus' words in Mark 3:29-30," she read slowly. "There Jesus says, 'Whoever blasphemes against the Holy Spirit never has forgiveness, but is guilty of an eternal sin.'" As she read, a puzzled look ran across the face of her brother. "The unforgivable sin applies to those who, after knowledge, deliberately and persistently reject Christ and refuse to recognize his work as the work of God," April continued. "The essence of this sin is to pervert the whole spiritual order and thus to disqualify oneself from the kingdom of righteousness."

When April was finished, it was August's turn. "I guess April and I read the same sources," he said carefully. "I was about to say that by persisting in this sin people lose the capacity to accept God's free offer of grace." Then he turned to David. "Pastor, why do you want us to study a passage from Mark when we are going to study Matthew this morning?"

"Excellent question," David responded. "You and April have commented on the passage from Mark that we traditionally associate with the 'unforgivable sin.' I believe Matthew has another version. It is similar to the phrase from the Lord's Prayer, 'Forgive us our sins as we forgive those who sin against us.' It almost sounds like being forgiven and forgiving are tied together, doesn't it?"

David then began to read the gospel. He put a strong emphasis on the words "Not seven times, but, I tell you, seventy *times* seven," and again, "So my heavenly Father will also do to everyone of you, if you do not forgive your brother or sister from your heart" (Matthew 18:35).

"Peter thought he was being very generous in suggesting that he forgive his brother or sister seven times," David said. "In fact, he went further than Jewish law demanded. Jesus wants forgiveness to overflow, he says 'seventy times seven times.' In other words, forgiveness without limits.

"The next story (Matthew 18:23-35) underlines his message. A king had a servant who owed him millions of dollars. The passage says 10,000 talents. The annual income of Herod the Great, Israel's king, was 900 talents, so you can see there was no way the servant could ever repay that amount. Out of compassion the king forgave him."

David saw April and August staring at the floor. "Next, the man who was forgiven insisted that a friend repay him 100 denarii, which may have been worth about $30. When his friend pleaded for mercy, the man refused and threw him into jail. When the king heard what happened, he arrested the first servant. The story ends with these words, 'So my heavenly Father will also do to every one of you, if you do not forgive your brother or sister from your heart.'" David concluded, "I think we may have another unforgivable sin."

There was an awkward silence until one of the women in the front row responded, "I don't understand," she said. "This story and your point aren't clear to me."

David resisted saying anything more. He let the words hang in the air. Finally a man's voice broke the silence. "It is painfully clear to me." It was August.

"God is like the king," he said slowly, without looking up. "God looks at the dark hearts of his servants, the debt people like you and me owe. There is no way we can repay him. We cry out, 'Lord have mercy, Christ have mercy.' And in Christ's death on the cross God forgives our massive debt to him, a debt worth millions. But when we meet a sister who owes us a few lousy bucks, we refuse to forgive that sister." August glanced across the room briefly catching April's eye. "We refuse to pass on the very forgiveness of the king, a forgiveness that allows us to walk free and live clear. The unforgivable sin is refusing to forgive as we have been forgiven. I'm afraid it is all too clear."

When August finished, no one else spoke. The only sounds were a nervous cough and the noise of people changing positions on their hard metal chairs. Finally August stood up and walked out of the room. No one moved until the bell rang, calling people to worship. August was not in his usual spot when the service began.

David thought about August during the entire service, and again on Monday, Tuesday, and Wednesday. He continually second-guessed his decision to go public with their family feud. At the time, he had decided it would take a terrible jolt to make them see. He also knew that their division was not essentially private, but something that touched the lives of the entire congregation.

David thought about visiting his friend, but decided to wait for August to make the first move. On Friday, August did. David looked up from his desk and saw him standing silently in the doorway. David wordlessly invited him in. For several minutes the two men sat looking at each other without speaking.

Finally August's eyes narrowed. "That was a dirty trick you pulled on me Sunday," he said. Then there was a long pause. "But I deserved it. This has been a long week. It has been a time of soul searching. You said nothing new, nothing I didn't know. I knew all about forgiveness as a concept, an idea. For mercy sakes, I've led classes on the subject. My problem is that I knew little of forgiveness as an experience."

August thought for a moment before he continued. "I visited the girls last night. I told them I had been a fool. I told them their friendship was worth more than trinkets, whether those trinkets be new or antique. I asked them to pray for me. We all cried a lot before I left."

Tears flowed down August's wrinkled cheeks. "Pastor, I have sinned. Pray for me," he cried.

David walked over to his friend and asked, "Is this your confession?" August nodded.

David put his hands on the old man's head and spoke lovingly, "Almighty God, in his mercy, has given his Son to die for you. As a called and ordained minister of the church of Christ and by his authority, I therefore declare to you the entire forgiveness of all your sins, in the name of the God who forgives, seventy times seven times."

Two Farmers

This story is based on a fable by Leo Tolstoy.

Two farmers were driving their tractors, pulling wagons filled with produce, when they attempted to pass each other on a narrow road. When their trailers became entangled, one cried to the other, "Move aside. I must get to market immediately."

The other farmer shouted back, "You move. I am in a hurry to get home."

For a long time they shouted at each other. A third farmer who was listening to the dispute finally said, "If each of you would move over just one foot, you could both get to your destination sooner."

The Oak and the Reeds

Scholars are convinced that Aesop's fables, originally written in ancient Greece, were shaped by Christian monks during the Middle Ages. This is one of Aesop's fables.

A very large oak tree was uprooted by the wind, thrown across a stream, and fell among some reeds. "I wonder," said the oak, "how you, who are so light and weak, are not crushed by strong winds."

The reeds replied, "You fight the wind rigidly, and consequently are destroyed. We, on the other hand, bend before the least breath of air, and remain unbroken."

"Everyone who humbles himself will be exalted, and those who exalt themselves will be humbled" (Matthew 23:12).

Little Girls Wiser *than* Parents

This is adapted from a story by Leo Tolstoy.

Easter had come that year before the snow was gone. In a new subdivision two little girls, Amy and Rachel, just back from morning worship, decided to show each other their new clothes. As the two girls walked, they tried to avoid the puddles on their still unpaved street. Finally the temptation was too strong and Amy announced that she planned to jump in the mud puddle.

"First let's take off our shoes," Rachel advised, "so our mothers won't get mad." Quickly the girls removed socks and shoes and began to carefully wade in the water. "We can't get our dresses dirty," Rachel reminded her friend.

No sooner had she spoken than Amy plopped one foot in the puddle, splashing water all over Rachel's face and dress. Rachel quickly retaliated by stomping in the water to splash on Amy but managed to get herself even dirtier.

Just then, Rachel's mother came to get her for lunch. What she saw was her daughter dripping with mud. "What happened?" she screamed.

"Amy splashed me on purpose," Rachel cried in her own defense. Quickly Rachel's mother seized Amy, giving her a blow on the backside. Amy let out a cry, which was heard by her mother.

"Why did you hit my child?" she shouted at her neighbor. The women's quarrel grew more heated with every word. Soon the fathers joined in the fray. Everyone was shouting; no one was listening. Then someone suddenly pushed someone else and a punch was thrown.

Meanwhile, Rachel went back to the puddle. She picked up a stone and began scraping the earth to let the puddle run into the street. While she was digging, Amy came and started helping her form a little canal with a chip of wood.

Just as the pushing began, the girls' canal released the water into the street. It ran right to the spot where the men were shouting and pushing each other. The girls began to chase the water, running on opposite sides of the rivulet.

"Catch it Amy. Catch it!" Rachel shouted. Giggling, the two girls chased the chip of wood, which floated with the water, right into the midst of the men. One of the girls' grandmothers took both youngsters by the arm and said to the men, "You are fighting over these two girls who have forgotten everything long ago and are playing happily together. They are wiser than you!"

The men looked at the girls and hung their heads. Then they shook hands and went back to their own houses.

Unless you become like little children,
you will not enter the kingdom of heaven.

Easter *at the* Boondocks

This was first told on an Easter Sunday.

David Zwanziger believes that events, not people, write Easter sermons. He came to this conclusion the first year he was a pastor in Blackhawk.

Easter arrived just three months after David graduated from seminary and was installed as pastor of Maple Street Church. He completed his sermonic creation early Saturday morning and told his wife, Doris, "Behold, it is very good."

Doris smiled, "So you like your sermon. What is it about?"

"I based it on some ideas from the great theologian Paul Tillich," David explained. "He says the resurrection is the symbol that estrangement from our authentic self is over. God has made possible the New Being, and if humans will just accept their acceptance, unauthentic existence ends and new life begins."

Doris shook her head, but David didn't notice. "Actually, it isn't a totally new sermon. I preached something like it in seminary, and my classmates thought it was great."

Early Saturday evening David drove the family car to church where the members of the church youth group were practicing their parts for the sunrise service. When rehearsal was over, Rich Peterson, who the kids call "Tiny" because he is 6-foot-5-inches and in the ninth grade, said, "Pastor, can you give me a ride home?"

David replied, "I don't know where you live, Tiny."

The tall lad replied, "No problem, I know where I live."

The Peterson home, located at the end of Pleasant Ridge, was easy to find with Tiny providing directions. Once David became his own navigator, sailing into a sea of darkness, he couldn't remember whether to turn right at the end of the cement, and left at the cross roads, or the other way around. It had taken only ten minutes to reach the

Peterson farm. Twenty minutes after David waved good-bye to the tall youngster he was still driving down a deserted dirt road, totally lost. When the engine sputtered he knew he was also out of gas.

David was overcome with anxiety. It was ten o'clock on Holy Saturday, he had failed to tell Doris where he was going, he had to be at church at six o'clock the next morning, and he was lost.

He got out of the car, kicked the tires, and began to walk. Ten minutes later he came to a fork in the road and saw lights, lots of lights, up ahead to the right. As he drew closer he could see it was a bar. Soon he could read the neon sign that said, "THE BOONDOCKS." Everyone, including someone new to the community like David, knew that the Boondocks was one of the seediest taverns in the county.

When he arrived the first thing he saw was a bunch of rusty cars and pickup trucks. As he walked to the door his eyes fell on six shiny motorcycles. Both groups of vehicles made him nervous. Inside he could hear the jukebox playing a Merle Haggard number. He took a deep breath and walked in the front door.

The rancid smell of spilled beer and smoke filled the air. David looked around and didn't recognize anyone. He wasn't sure whether this was good or bad. He wondered what his members would think if they heard he had spent Holy Saturday at the Boondocks.

He walked to the bar aware that every eye in the house was on him. "What'll ya have?" the bartender asked.

What David wanted was a ride home—fast, but he found himself saying, "I'll have a Coke." The bartender frowned. Evidently there were not a lot of soft drinks consumed at the Boondocks.

Over in a corner a few men in leather jackets were shooting pool. David walked over intending to ask about a ride into town, but before he knew it, he was in the midst of a game. David's father, who sold sporting equipment, had taught him to play pool at age six. Normally he was a good player. That night he was excellent. Everything went in. Twice he ran the table off the break. One of the guys said, "You ought to play Turk."

The call went out across the room, "Turk, we've got a hotshot over here." David watched as a man who stood about 5-feet-8-inches and weighed a bit over 250 pounds, got up, took off his leather jacket, gently removed his cue from a case, and growled, "Set 'em up."

Turk was good, but that night David was better. When David beat him three games in a row, the big man snarled, "Shark, you're too good for me. I'll buy you a drink." David ordered another Coke and sat down, realizing he had won admiration and a new name, "Shark."

Soon the inevitable question came, "Whadda ya do, Shark?"

David took a deep breath. Should he tell the truth or should he lie? Lying seemed safer, but it was Holy Saturday. "I'm a minister over in Blackhawk," he said reluctantly.

There was shocked silence around the table before people began to laugh. "We got ourselves a preacher." "Hey, this fella makes house calls." "Welcome to St. Boondocks. This ought to increase business on Saturday night."

Suddenly a voice silenced the crowd. "Shaddup!" It was Turk. "Some of us more sensitive types want to talk religion." The mood changed immediately. One by one, the men told their story. Some had gone through confirmation but hadn't been to church in years. Others told how church members treated them with contempt. They were certain they wouldn't be welcome at worship. Finally it was Turk's turn.

"Me, I've never been to church," he said looking at the table. "My mom never got married, so when I was born people told her she wasn't good enough for any church around here. I've never been to Sunday school either. All I've learned about the Bible is from TV. I've seen the movie on the Ten Commandments four or five times. Still, I don't know much." He looked sadly at David and concluded, "I don't even know what Easter's about."

There was silence. Eyes shifted to the pastor. He realized Turk had offered him an invitation. Should he tell them about the New Being, about estrangement and authentic selfhood? He looked into the faces of the men in leather jackets and began, "Jesus was born in a little town 2,000 years ago. His mother wasn't married at the time. Later when he became a preacher, people used this against him. They asked how God could speak through a man who came from a questionable background, but it was clear God did speak to and through him."

David continued, "During his life Jesus traveled from town to town teaching and healing. The folks who were rich and famous had little to do with him. He enjoyed the company of those who respectable folks called sinners. Many of his closest friends were despised by the rest of society. The stories he told often surprised people, because they told how, in God's eyes, many of the folks who society considered to be bad were actually close to God. He taught that God loved everyone, rich and poor alike. He taught that we are all brothers and sisters."

David took a sip of Coke and continued. "During most of his life Jesus lived in the northern part of Israel, a rather backward place by some standards. After three years of preaching in the north, he decided to head south to the capital, Jerusalem. When he entered the Holy City on Palm Sunday, thousands of people greeted him like a hero. They tore branches from the trees and called him a king. It was the kind of parade we have for Super Bowl champs."

David went on, saying, "As the popularity of Jesus grew, so did the opposition from the people in power. They managed to bribe one of his disciples, Judas, toward the middle of that week, to discover where they could find Jesus alone. While he was praying in a garden on Thursday night, soldiers came and arrested him. They tried him in a court, but the trial was crooked. The religious leaders wanted him out of the way so bad that they lied. He was found guilty and sentenced to death. The soldiers put a royal garment on him, made a crown out of thorns, and put it on his head. Then they fell down and mocked him saying, 'Hail! King of the Jews!' Finally they nailed his hands and feet to a wooden cross and crucified him. It was a death reserved only for the worst enemies of the state. Normally crucifixion lasted from three days to a week."

David paused and looked at his congregation. He had seldom had such an attentive audience. He continued. "As Jesus hung in the 90 to 100 degree sun, nearly all of his friends, his disciples, ran away. Only one of his male companions, along with a few women who followed him, remained. Within three hours, this gentle, loving man died. They took him down and a stranger put his body in a small cave."

Tears clouded the eyes of several of the men at the table. "It looked like the authorities had won. It appeared that they had silenced him. It looked like another victory for the system. That was a Friday. Early Sunday morning three women, including Mary Magdalene, a woman some people think had once been a prostitute, went to the cave to visit him. They found that even though soldiers had guarded it, the body of

Jesus was gone. Suddenly an angel appeared and told them that Jesus was alive, not dead. Filled with both fear and joy, the women hurried away, only to be met by Jesus himself. He told them to go tell his friends who were in hiding that he was alive and that he would meet them soon."

Turk interrupted him, saying, "Shark, you mean to tell me Jesus would still speak to those dirty bums? Pardon me, but they were rotten. They left him when he needed them most."

David nodded. "That is the kind of man he is. He treats people like God treats us. God loves us even when we are unfaithful. Even when we forget or ignore him. God forgives us even when we betray him. That is why we call his teaching *gospel*, which means, 'good news.'"

Turk shook his head, "Shark, that's a crazy story."

David replied, "Turk, this is a crazy world. Our God turns losing into winning. Jesus teaches that what many think is weakness is really strength. Jesus declared that people who some treat as unclean are often God's closest friends. Jesus spent his life loving and serving people, not using force. By raising Jesus from death, God said, 'The way of Jesus is my way.' Furthermore, Jesus gives us a promise. If we believe in him, we will never die. We will live with him."

One of the men in the back said, "I remember something we memorized in Sunday school about that. 'For God so loved the world that he gave his only son that whosoever believes in him will not perish, but have everlasting life.'"

David nodded. "That just about sums it all up."

A few minutes later David told Turk about his car problem. Turk said, "We'll have you going in no time."

"But there are no gas stations open," David said.

"No problem, Shark," Turk replied, "I've got me a siphon." A few minutes later, after a brief visit with a pickup parked in back of the bar, David had enough gas, along with good directions, to get home.

Doris, of course, was worried sick. David told her, "You'll never believe what happened to me."

And she didn't.

Doris said, "You better get some sleep. You have to be up by 4:30."

David shook his head, "I have to rewrite my sermon." He figured if a sermon wouldn't preach at the Boondocks on Holy Saturday, it wouldn't preach at the church on Easter Sunday. He turned the lights off and went to bed about 2 A.M.

The next morning he didn't talk about the New Being or estrangement from authentic selfhood. He simply told the story of the death and resurrection of Jesus, how God raised Jesus from death and gave him and all of us new life and hope.

People said the sermon was good, but what really got them talking was the strange group of visitors who parked six shiny motorcycles in front of the church and sat in one of the front pews. When one of the ushers asked who they were, a big man who looked most uncomfortable in his suit growled, "We're friends of Shark."

The Holy Week Visitor

On Maundy Thursday evening, about ten o'clock, Pam Nesheim breathed a sigh of relief and sat down at the piano. It had been a long day and she had finally managed to get the children to bed. Her husband, Rick, a nervous wreck for most of Holy Week, was upstairs working on his Good Friday sermon. Rick, who never looked forward to preaching, found Holy Week—with its four sermons in eight days—pure torture. Playing the piano was a release for Pam, who worried whenever Rick worried. Did he really have the stuff to be a pastor?

As Pam began to play Moonlight Sonata, she heard a noise near the back of the house and then a door open noisily. Pam leaped from the piano, dashed to the kitchen, and discovered a small man with a very large beard weaving into the room. He knocked over a chair and leaned on the kitchen sink. Melanchthon, the Nesheims' large dog, wagged his tail and began to lick the stranger's hand. Pam edged her way to the stairs and tried not to sound as frightened as she felt. "Rick," she pleaded, "could you come down here? Immediately! We have a guest."

By the time Rick got downstairs, he found the guest sitting at the kitchen table, quite confused and quite intoxicated. Melanchthon had his shaggy head buried in the man's lap. "Rick," Pam said, "do you know Delbert Matson?"

"People call me 'Fuzzy,'" the man mumbled. "Yer wife tells me this is the parsonage. You ain't lived here too long."

"Just over four years," Rick replied.

"I'm an atheist!" Fuzzy said emphatically.

At that moment Rick was more concerned about the man's sobriety and the occasion of the visit than he was his faith. "What brings you out our way?" he asked.

"I think I'm headed home."

"Where is home?" Rick inquired.

"About half a mile south of the Lyon farm on County Trunk B."

"You must be a neighbor of Marie Parker."

"Neighbor! I'm her brother. Moved in with her five years ago when Milt died. Horrible thing it was too. That's another reason I ain't a believer. Why'd he do a thing like that to Milt? Left Marie with a big farm and no kids to help. You call that fair?" Fuzzy shook his finger at the pastor to accent his sentences.

Marie Parker, a small woman who sat two rows from the back in church each Sunday, always looked tired. Rick knew she was a widow who farmed alone, but he had no idea that she lived with a brother.

Pam, who had left the room to check on the children, reentered. "Delbert, I don't see a car outside. How did you get here?" The parsonage was located on a small hill about a quarter of a mile from their rural church and over a half mile from the nearest family.

Fuzzy looked puzzled, "I was driving when I left the Boondocks. I've really got myself in hot water this time. Marie will be ashamed of me again."

Pam looked at Rick with alarm. The Boondocks, a seedy bar, was more than six miles from their home. Rather than find out more about transportation she asked, "Who would like coffee?"

"We both would," Rick answered. Pam was surprised. Rick had never drunk a cup of coffee in the ten years she knew him. Later, when the story was finally told, she discovered Fuzzy didn't drink coffee either. That night both drank for the sake of the other.

As they sat around the kitchen table, Fuzzy told his story. His father died when he was eleven. All through high school and for two years after graduation, Fuzzy worked with Doc Benson, a veterinarian. In order to avoid the army, he enlisted in the navy and a year later was assigned duty in Vietnam.

One day in Vietnam, he and a buddy, Goose, were riding watch on a small boat traveling up a river looking for snipers, when a sniper found Goose. "The day they sent Goose home in a bag I got drunk and stayed that way until they sent me home," he cried.

"You must have been frightened to death," Rick said, absorbed in the story.

"Frightened, powerfully lonely, and mad," Fuzzy insisted. "Nobody understood that I had lost my best friend. Nobody cared that I had only one good buddy and he was dead. Right then and there I decided not to believe in God anymore. And I haven't."

"Do you blame God for the death of Goose?" Pam asked.

"I blame everybody. As for God, he's either dead or he just doesn't want to get involved."

For nearly an hour Fuzzy poured out one bitter story after another. He told of employers, neighbors, and friends who turned against him once he came home. He was critical of everyone but Marie.

When Fuzzy seemed to be more alert, Rick took his guest home. Marie came to the door, saw her brother standing with her pastor and cried, "Fuzzy, every day you find a new way to embarrass me."

Before Rick left that night, he offered to help Fuzzy search for his pickup truck in the morning. At Fuzzy's request, Rick arrived at the Parker place, about 7 A.M., before too many people were on the road. They found the pickup three miles from the parsonage, keys in the ignition and the gas tank on empty. It was nearly ten o'clock by the time they gassed up the old truck and waved good-bye.

That night as he stood greeting people at the door for Good Friday services, Rick saw Marie accompanied by a small man in a suit. It was Fuzzy. As he entered the church, he whispered to Rick, "Don't get your hopes up. I'm doing this for Marie."

The sermon for Good Friday was based on the words of Jesus: "My God, my God, why have you forsaken me?" Rick told the people that the cross was a place of loneliness for God, who lost his only son.

"The cross is a sign of God's solidarity with all the abandoned of the world," the pastor continued. "Sin separates us from others and God. The cross unites us."

Sugar Valley Lutheran Church, where Rick serves, is on the edge of the unincorporated village of Prairie. The village consists of a grocery store, café, tavern, and about 190 people.

By Saturday morning, when Rick stopped by Plante's Grocery, all 190 people knew the story of the pastor's Thursday night visitor. "Heard you worked late Thursday night," Gover Plante said cheerfully as Rick entered the store. Before he left a half-dozen people stopped him to tell a Fuzzy story. A kind and gentle man before he went into the service, Fuzzy was radically different when he returned from Vietnam. "He can't keep a job, Pastor," one man confided. "When something goes wrong, and it always does, it is always someone else's fault. Each time people fire him he gets more bitter."

"I always thought he ought to be a veterinarian," a woman whispered. "There isn't an animal in the county that won't lay at his feet." Rick smiled to think of Melanchthon's quiet greeting.

On Easter, Fuzzy was in church again, and again he went out of his way to speak to Rick. "An hour listening to your nonsense is a small price to pay for peace at home," Fuzzy explained.

As Rick told the story of Easter from Mark's gospel, he focused on the angel's message to the women, "Go, tell his disciples and Peter that he will meet them in Galilee, just as he told them."

"Even though Peter and the disciples had betrayed and denied Jesus, he still kept his promise to them. Easter hope is even for those who deny God," Rick said.

During communion, Fuzzy sat alone. He was the only person in the white frame church who did not come to the altar.

The Monday after Easter, as was her custom, Pam's mom arrived to take care of the children, allowing Rick and Pam to get away for a couple days. On Thursday morning, his first day back in the office, Rick saw a familiar pickup turn into the church's parking lot. It was Fuzzy.

Rick met him at the door and invited him in. Instead of entering, Fuzzy pushed his yellow "Renk's Seeds" cap back on his head and leaned against the wall. "You preachers ain't used to a normal work week, eh?" he said with a smile on his face. "Work three and take off three."

Rick thought about explaining that he always took a couple days off after Easter, but just smiled.

"I know you took aim at me last week," Fuzzy said, becoming more serious. "But it didn't work. I still don't believe. God is cruel. He lets too many good people die." Fuzzy stared at the pastor, letting his words sink in.

Rick didn't wait long to break the silence. "Don't you beat all, Fuzzy. You claim you don't believe in God and then get mad at him. You sure burn up a lot of energy being angry at someone who doesn't exist."

Fuzzy squinted his eyes and stared at the pastor with a puzzled expression.

Rick spoke softly. "Fuzzy, I know a terrible thing happened in Vietnam, but you've been mad at the wrong person for a lot of years. I wasn't taking aim at you on Good Friday, but this much I'll tell you, your heart wasn't the only one that broke when Goose was killed. The cross is God's way of participating in all of the murder and pain in this world."

Neither man spoke for a long time. Then Rick said quietly, "I expect that someday you'll face God when you face yourself, including your drinking."

Fuzzy didn't reply. He just stared impassively at the pastor. Then he turned, walked to the pickup truck, and drove away.

When he got home that night, Rick told Pam, "I'm afraid we've seen the last of Fuzzy for a while."

Rick was wrong. The next Sunday, Fuzzy was in church again. The next Monday, he was at the pastor's office again. This time when he was invited into the study, he entered wordlessly and sat down.

"I didn't have a very good day yesterday," he began. "In fact I didn't have a good night either. Part way through church, I figured out what was happening. It wasn't you aiming at me, it was God. He looked me straight in the eye and said, 'Put your finger here, and put your hand in my side. Don't be faithless, believe.' Not only did he say it once, he said it over and over again to me and Thomas."

Rick interrupted. "Who is Thomas?"

Fuzzy looked surprised. "You know, the disciple. Finally about midnight, both of us, me and Thomas, took him up on his offer and stuck our hand into his wound. When I pulled mine out it was dripping blood. Before you could blink, me and Thomas cried out together, 'My Lord and my God.'"

The little man began to cry. Then he sobbed. Finally he looked up and said, "I'm ready to get help. Please."

The next eight months were both difficult and fruitful for Fuzzy. Two days after he left Pastor Nesheim's office he entered a detoxification program. He was ready. He was ready to stop blaming others, including God, for what had happened. He was ready to listen to others, particularly at Alcoholics Anonymous meetings, which he attended faithfully. "I'm willing to trust a power greater than myself," he told Rick. He was also ready to be a part of a community which he found at Sugar Valley.

January and February were rocky, but in April Fuzzy was hired as assistant to a young vet. The young doctor was patient and said that there is improvement in Fuzzy's work habits.

One Tuesday, roughly a year after their first encounter, Rick approached his new friend with a request. "The story of Thomas is the gospel again for the Sunday after Easter. I wondered if you would be willing to read it in church."

Fuzzy responded immediately. "Nah. I'm not the reading type. But I'll give you this, it has become my favorite story. It's a wonderful invitation from the Lord for us to turn from doubt to faith. Maybe this year someone else will put their hand in the Lord's side."

CHAPTER III

Faith, Hope,
and
Promise

Moses *and the* Prophets

On the Monday Evie Knutson knocked on her pastor's office door, she felt like she had spent the weekend riding an emotional rollercoaster. It all began the previous Friday when she took her twelve-year-old son, Joel, to her father's farm for the weekend.

Two years ago Joel's grandfather, Cyrus Vig, bought him a beautiful show horse, Black Magic, to entice his only grandson to visit him more often. It worked. From the day he received the horse, Joel began to spend all of his spare hours, including most of the summer, at the Vig Ranch riding and grooming the impressive animal. Last Friday, with the county fair only a week away, Joel needed the weekend to put his horse through its final paces.

Cy Vig had been his small town's most respected attorney for nearly forty years. In addition to his practice as a leading trial lawyer, Cy had made a small fortune in real estate. When his wife died, he went into semi-retirement and built a new home on the ranch. He left the old house for Chris Lawton, from whom he had purchased the farm nearly fifteen years earlier. Chris, a gentle, quiet man, had the skills necessary to keep the buildings in good repair.

Before Evie left the ranch on Friday, she told her father she would be back to pick up Joel the next day. As always, Cy bargained for more time. "Why don't you let the boy stay the weekend? I'll bring him home Sunday afternoon."

"Daddy, you know perfectly well why I'm coming after Joel tomorrow," Evie replied. "That is the only way I am sure he will be in church Sunday morning. I'll get old waiting for you to join us."

Cy laughed. Religion was the only area of disagreement Cy had with his beloved daughter. "I told you I'd start going to church when God sends me a sign. In fact, Evangeline, if you are going to come up with a miracle, it better be soon. I'm not getting any younger."

"You're only getting more stubborn. I'm not sure you'd recognize a sign if it fell on your head," she said before she drove away.

The following afternoon, at precisely 2 P. M., Evie, along with her husband, Lyle, arrived at the ranch, where they found Cy sitting on his rocker in his screened-in-porch, watching Joel and Magic conclude their rehearsal. "They have become a real team," Cy announced with pride. "If Joel rides this well next weekend, you'll be living with a grand champion."

A few minutes later, Joel rode by the porch. "Hi, Mom! Hi, Dad! I'm going to take Magic for a short run before we go. I won't be long."

Without waiting for a reply, he raced toward the field and circled back. He was heading toward the barn when a chipmunk darted in front of the galloping horse, causing it to rear up, throwing Joel headlong toward the ground.

For a moment the three figures on the porch froze in fear. Then the old man began to run toward the still body of his grandson, his daughter and son-in-law close behind. From that moment on events became a blur for Evie. She remembers pushing Lyle back toward the house and shouting, as if he were deaf, "Call the hospital." And she remembers her father overruling her, "It will be quicker to call Doctor Swiggum; he lives only a mile away." She remembers the doctor arriving, after what seemed an eternity, and she remembers his skilled hands moving, touching, probing. Finally she remembers the doctor turning, the color drained from his face and whispering, "There's no heartbeat."

What Evie doesn't remember is when Chris appeared. Had he been there from the beginning? She became aware of him shortly after the doctor's terrifying words. The old man took Evie and Lyle gently by the hand, motioned to Cy, and pulled them all to their knees. He then placed his hands on the boy's head, let out a great sigh, and began to pray. It was a simple prayer, "Jesus, you gave life to the son of the widow of Nain. You can give life to Joel. Please, do it now."

Then he was silent. The only sounds Evie remembers were the pounding of her heart and her father's labored breathing. Finally, after several minutes, Chris spoke quietly to Dr. Swiggum, "I'd be obliged if you'd check the boy again."

Dr. Swiggum meekly responded and immediately let out a gasp. "I can hear a heartbeat." At that moment the rescue squad appeared, and the lad was lifted onto a stretcher and taken to the hospital, with the family following close behind in Lyle's car.

Less than an hour after they arrived at the hospital, Dr. Swiggum walked into the waiting room wearing a weary smile. "He is resting comfortably and wants to see you. By the way, I couldn't answer one of his questions. He wants to know who took care of Magic."

Late that night, after spending the evening with a tired but talkative Joel, Evie drove Cy back to the ranch. "What time do you figure to go into the hospital tomorrow morning?" Cy asked his daughter.

Looking at Lyle, Evie shrugged. "I'll probably relieve Lyle about seven. Then we'll go to early church and thank God for our miracle." She shyly asked her father, "Do you want to join us?"

"I think I'll sit this one out," Cy said as he got out of the backseat. He paused a moment before he spoke. "Doesn't it beat all how a fine physician like Dr. Swiggum missed that heartbeat? Well, we can thank our lucky stars for the rescue team." With that he leaned over, kissed his daughter and headed into the house.

Evie started Sunday on a high. Filled with gratitude she arrived at the hospital before dawn. Two hours later, she left for church convinced that Joel was a living miracle. Before worship, she hugged shy old Chris until the man blushed scarlet. During the announcements she shared her joy with the entire congregation.

As the afternoon wore on Evie's thoughts turned from Joel to Cy, and frustration began to build. For years she had prayed that God would break through her father's cold analytical soul and fan the flames of faith. She had often pleaded with him to join the three of them for worship. "You'll like the pastor. He is a good preacher. Just come to church a few Sundays to see what you think."

Then a few months ago, during one of their frequent arguments about religion, Cy said, "I don't see a lot of evidence that God is involved in this world. What I need is a sign, a miracle." Then he laughed. "I'd like to have it be as big a sign as possible. Maybe something like God writing my name in fire across the sky." Then he became serious again. "I guess my favorite theologian is Woody Allen. He once said that God isn't dead; it is just that he is an underachiever."

From that moment Evie began to pray for a miracle. Day after day she asked God to reveal himself to her father.

As they sat in the hospital, she thought that all her prayers had been answered. Joel was alive and her father's wish had been granted. Only when she took him home Saturday evening did she realize that Cy had missed the sign. All Sunday she wondered what had gone wrong. Finally, late in the afternoon, she drove out to the ranch and attempted to help her father understand what had happened, only to have him say something about the marvels of modern medicine.

Now on Monday morning, Evie decided to take her dilemma to her friend. Maybe he could help her sort things out. What had gone wrong? Was there something more she could do?

For nearly thirty minutes the young pastor listened as Evie cried and laughed her way through the amazing events of the previous Saturday. He shared her joy and her agony. Finally he spoke. "What a tremendous miracle you have experienced. You must have felt like the father of the prodigal. 'My son was dead and is alive. He was lost and is found.' I understand your deep disappointment. For such a long time you have wanted your father to share your faith in God. You thought Joel's miracle was the event that would begin his faith journey."

Evie nodded. "Precisely. What went wrong?"

David considered his words carefully. "I need to say several things. First, I feel some sympathy for your father. It isn't easy to discern when God is acting in this world. I am rather skeptical of miraculous healing claims. There are a lot of claims made by religious people that don't look like miracles to me either."

Evie's eyes narrowed. "But I saw this with my own eyes. Dad saw what I saw."

"That leads me to a second point," David said carefully. "I'm afraid that miracles don't produce faith as much as they reassure it. Only believers see the miracle. Without faith the miracle is missed. Unbelievers can find a dozen alternate explanations. A seminary professor of mine used to say, 'If a man fell off a ten-story building and landed on his feet, one or two people would say, 'God be praised.' The rest would say, 'Do it again, slowly.'"

Evie looked confused. "What about all of the miracles of Jesus? Didn't they lead people to faith?"

"A few, but often people observed miracles as if they were spiritually blind. The Old Testament says that when God performed his miracles in Egypt, Pharaoh's heart was hard."

He thought for a few second before he continued. "There is a story in the Gospel of Luke about a rich man who died and went to hell. He looked up and saw Lazarus, a beggar who had once eaten his garbage, sitting next to Abraham in heaven. The rich man first requested that Lazarus visit him in hell to provide relief. When his request was refused, he asked that Lazarus be sent with a warning to his brothers who were still living. Abraham told him that everything necessary for faith was still available—the writings of Moses and the Prophets. 'No, Father Abraham, the rich man said; but if some one goes to them from the dead, they will repent.' Abraham disagreed and said, 'If they don't hear Moses and the Prophets, neither will they be convinced if some one should rise from the dead.'"

The pastor smiled. "Jesus had already performed many signs. He had brought sight to the blind, made deaf people hear and walked on the water. Still the religious leaders resisted him. It is the same today. God's signs and wonders are here in abundance, but we attribute his work to chance, luck, and modern medicine."

"If something as powerful as a miracle doesn't work, what will?" Evie asked somewhat exasperated.

"The Word. That is what Jesus meant by 'Moses and the Prophets.' The Word—written, spoken, shared—has tremendous power. When we hear the Word we are brought into the presence of God. Even human words can be powerful. They can heal, comfort, and express love. Or they can curse and criticize. You know how deeply people have been hurt by a word spoken in anger."

Evie nodded. Her eyes told him to continue.

"God's word is even more powerful," the pastor explained. "They used the Greek word *dunamis*, from which we get 'dynamite' to describe the effects of God's word. In the beginning God said, 'Let there be light,' and a world was formed. When Jesus spoke people were healed or forgiven, silenced or confounded. The Word is not mere noise. It is our present experience of God. When we listen to the Word we are put in touch with the living God. The Word— written, spoken, sung, prayed—is the presence of Jesus. That is why worship and Bible study are so important. One more thing, your love for your father is a silent sermon about the love of God. Most of the best words are lived rather than said."

"As I think about it, a lot of people who witnessed the miracles of Jesus drew another conclusion," Evie reflected. "People didn't even come to faith when he was raised from the dead." She thought for a while. "What do I do now?"

"That is really my question to you. What do you do now?"

Evie laughed. "Always the counselor who makes people solve their own problems, right? Well, I continue to give thanks to God for bringing my son back to life."

The pastor agreed.

"And I continue to pray for Father. After all, prayer was the vehicle for Joel's miracle. What brought life to Joel can bring life to Cy."

The pastor said, "I think Cy is mighty fortunate that he has a daughter who loves him enough to keep praying for him. And Joel is lucky to have a mom who has allowed herself to be fed by God's word. I'd like to be a prayer partner with you. I'll remember your father every day. Perhaps we can start right now."

And they did.

The Choice

David Zwanziger likes being a minister. He not only likes preaching, he enjoys preparing sermons. Though his thirteen- and fourteen-year-olds can be a test, he looks forward to confirmation. David, unlike most other pastors, even likes wedding rehearsals. He enjoys watching the dynamics of two families about to merge together.

The only thing David dislikes about his profession is his monthly visit to the Women's Missionary Society. The reason—Gladys Olson.

Whenever David and Gladys are at the same meeting sparks fly. They are known to disagree over everything from trivial matters to issues of great import. The subject on Tuesday was discipleship.

When David finished his very brief meditation, Gladys announced that she was moved to make a few observations. David grimaced. He knew from experience that she was about to "correct" everything he had just said. "Ours is a heavy burden, isn't it pastor?" she began. "We are called to take up our cross and follow Jesus. The way is narrow that leads to salvation. God has called many to work in his kingdom, but only a few have answered, 'Here am I, send me.' Others have chosen to participate in the pleasures of the world, but we have chosen to give up those pleasures in order to follow Jesus."

Gladys's comments on the pastor's remarks continued for ten minutes—five minutes longer than the devotions themselves. When she finished, David politely dismissed himself, walked slowly up the stairs muttering, closed the door to his office, and let out a primal cry. "ARAHHHHHHH!" He felt better.

At noon, David relieved a bit of his frustration by running with Curt Norton. About a mile from where they began Curt let out a scream. "For the love of God, David, can we run our normal pace?" David apologized and slowed down.

David had first met Curt in a seedy bar the night before Easter, three years earlier. While driving a boy home from a youth group meeting, David got lost, ran out of gas, and ended up in the Boondocks, where he met a motorcycle gang. Curt, a member of the gang, was a quiet kid who listened intently while David, at the invitation of Turk, told the Easter story. One and one-half years later, Curt wandered into David's office saying, "Pastor, I need help."

David soon learned that Curt, one of seven children, grew up in a home destroyed by alcohol. He lived part time with a father who drank at home and part time with a hot-tempered mother who spent her nights in a bar. "From the time we were in grade school we had to take care of ourselves," Curt told David. "We fed ourselves, went to bed on our own, and dressed ourselves in the morning. As soon as we reached sixteen, we left home. Most of us left the state. All the boys, except me, joined the service. And the girls got married. Only me and Jean, my youngest sister, graduated from high school."

At nineteen, while working at a cheese factory, Curt was introduced to pot. As the months passed, his use of marijuana increased. Everyone in his crowd, including his girlfriend, Cindy, either smoked or drank or did both, five to seven nights a week. One day his boss caught him smoking a joint on the job and he was fired. The next day he arrived at David's office.

"Pastor," Curt said crying. "Ever since that night in the bar, I've wanted to talk with you. But I was afraid. After yesterday, I'm afraid not to."

David introduced Curt to Ellis, a member of Narcotics Anonymous. Ellis took Curt to his first meeting the next evening. The following week Curt came to the church alone and sat in the back row in the corner. During the next year and a half, David measured Curt's progress by where he sat. "Today he moved up one row and in two seats," David told Doris after church. Before a year had passed, he was sitting in the middle of the congregation.

One of the turning points took place when Curt attended a men's retreat. The next Sunday he moved up three rows. In January one of the men in the congregation hired him at his sawmill. On Easter, after six months of instruction, he was baptized. As his friendships at church grew, his time with the old gang diminished. On Maundy Thursday, just three days before his baptism, he sold his cycle.

When the men finished their run, they stopped at the parsonage for a glass of water. Curt sat down on the deck as though he planned to stay. "I've been meaning to tell you that Cindy and I haven't been doing too well," he said simply. "Last night we called it quits."

David was caught off guard. "Curt, I'm sorry. What happened?"

"Well, it has been a long time coming," Curt explained. "She hasn't liked the way I've been changing. She says I ignore my old friends, and of course she's right. All along I thought we could work it out. We've been going together for three years and planned to get married. Last night she told me I had to choose between her and my new religion. I told her I cared for her more than she could ever know, but that the choice was simple. I had to choose God."

Curt smiled. "She said she didn't mean to make me chose between her and God, but her and the church. I told her I couldn't have one without the other."

David said, "You must be terribly sad."

Curt smiled bravely. "Pastor, it's crazy. One part of me is sad, but the other part of me is so full of joy I want to shout. I'm sad about losing Cindy. I still care about her. I still love her. But nothing can come between me and the life I have found these last few months, not even her. I'm clean. And the people at church have become the first real family I've ever had. I didn't want to choose, but if forced, I had to choose what is healthy. Actually, the choice was easy. My life with God is the most important thing in the whole world."

On Thursday David had coffee with Knute Lee, a retired pastor and dear friend. During coffee David shared the events of his week. David told him about Gladys before he shared Curt's story. "Sounds like it fits right into your sermon for Sunday," Knute said.

"You mean the pearl of great price?" David asked.

"Right," Knute responded, "that and the story of the treasure hidden in the field."

David nodded. "Like Curt, two men give up everything to possess the treasure or the pearl."

"And," Knute said, "they did it with joy. What they found overwhelmed them. It was worth everything they owned. They experienced a profound joy and were willing to sacrifice anything in order to have that pearl. The pearl, of course, is God or the Spirit of God."

"Which brings us to Gladys," David smiled.

"Poor Gladys," said Knute, shaking his head. "She has served God with a heavy heart for the thirty years I have known her. She is among the exasperated of the earth who feel burdened by their faith. She serves God because it is something she ought to do, something she *has* to do. Her life with God makes her miserable."

"And she in turns makes other people miserable," David added.

"It is a part of her understanding of evangelism," Knute said with a laugh. "It is called sharing the bad news."

"Curt, by contrast, serves God out of joy," David said.

Knute began to sing quietly, " 'I once was lost but now I'm found, was blind but now I see.' I've seen the pearl of great price re-enacted a dozen times in my life. Do you know Clayton Ross?"

"Of course," David responded, "he and Shelby are active members of First Methodist."

Knute stirred his coffee. "Well," he began, "I think if Jesus were telling about the kingdom today, he might use Clayton and Shelby's story. When Shelby went off to college, she almost broke Clayton's heart. They had dated since junior high. But she decided she didn't want to marry a farmer. Four months after she left, he followed her to the same college. He turned his wonderful, productive farm over to his brother and followed his heart. He was willing to give up anything for Shelby—his farm, his vocation, his home."

Knute poured another cup of coffee before he continued. "Well, Clayton decided that if he was going to pay for college he might as well learn something. He was on the dean's list the first semester. He had plenty of time to study because he didn't date or socialize much. He made it a point not to call or seek Shelby out. He knew she needed space. He went home on weekends to help his brother with chores and often brought back something for Shelby from her mother. He only spoke to her when they met in the hall, but he did send her a small gift on her birthday. He was available if she only looked his way. One day she did. Shelby was no fool. There are few men of the quality of Clayton. They started to date again. He told her, 'You are more important than the farm. I can do many things.' She didn't respond to that statement for nearly a month. Then one night she said, 'It doesn't make any difference what you do. I just want to be together.'"

David smiled. "Life with God is so full, so rich, that out of joy a person gives up all, including vocation, home, or romance, in order to possess it. That's not a bad start for a sermon. Too bad I can't use the stories."

"Well," Knute said, "maybe someone else can."

The Squabble

On Friday, David and Doris Zwanziger reluctantly returned home from vacation. They left home the day the children finished school, driving four hours to visit David's parents near Rhinelander, in northern Wisconsin. The elder Zwanzigers retired three years ago and built a new home next to a rustic old cottage that had served the family since David was three. They kept the cottage to entice their children and grandchildren to come visit.

Vacations for David meant three weeks of being a bum. He didn't shave, wear socks, or write sermons. Doris felt equal relief because her mother-in-law insisted on cooking for the brood and David and the grandparents provided most of the child-care. For the children a trip north meant swimming, fishing with Papa Zwanziger, and nightly trips to the Ice Cream Palace.

David hadn't been home fifteen minutes when the phone rang. It was Sigvald Munson, the slow-speaking church council president. Sigvald took so much time between sentences that during his calls David often thought the phone had gone dead. "Have you heard that we had a bit of a problem while you were gone?" the retired farmer began.

"Sigvald," David said with a trace of irritation, "we just got home. I haven't even brought the suitcases in from the car."

"Gladys Olson and Trygvie Lien had words after church three weeks ago," Sigvald continued, "and before you know it they were each in a corner with a group of cronies throwing daggers at the other. Pastor, you know between 'em they don't have enough tact to fill a hummingbird's beak."

David listened silently, nodding sadly. This had been building for over a year. They represented two different factions within the congregation. "Gladys wanted to have a special meeting of the church council, and when I said I didn't want to meet without you present, she convened the Women's Church Club. She's still president, you know."

There was a long pause before David spoke. "I have a lot to do yet tonight. Can you stop by the office in the morning and fill me in on the details?"

"It'd better be early," Sigvald said. "I'm certain both of them are planning to see you before noon. How about breakfast at Little Oslo?"

"That won't work," David said. "We will get interrupted by people stopping by to tell me that I sure have life easy, working one day a week and then taking a three-week vacation. Why don't you come over here about eight o'clock. We'll have breakfast on the porch."

When he hung up, David immediately told Doris the whole story. She listened quietly and asked, "What do you think set them off this time?"

"Let me see," he said counting on his fingers, "in the past they have argued over Nicaragua, the Nestle boycott, day-care, and banning *Playboy*. What is left, flag burning?"

Shortly after David arrived in Blackhawk, about five years ago, a few kids from the youth group asked him to look at some paintings that a controversial art teacher, a man who was a professed agnostic, had shown at school. Some people in the community were upset with the nudity in the pictures. When David supported the art teacher, a friendship developed. Soon the man, Trygvie Lien, joined the church, even though he told people he didn't accept the creeds that the church taught.

In an effort to get his new friend involved in congregational life, David invited Trygvie to design some posters for a hunger project. Soon Trygvie became a member of the social-action committee, and the church bulletin boards and hallways were filled with colorful posters educating people and urging action for a variety of social projects.

When some of Trygvie's posters were hung in a spot normally reserved for the women of the church, Gladys confronted Trygvie in the narthex. "Mr. Lien, you are rather new here. Do you know the difference between the church and a social service agency?"

After breakfast with Sigvald, David didn't know a whole lot more than he did the night before. All Sigvald could tell him was that the whole thing began with something about prayer and that there were several young couples who seemed to support Trygvie and a large number of older people, particularly women, who appeared to be on the side of Gladys.

The information that Sigvald lacked was soon available. When David arrived at his office, Gladys was waiting for him. Thirty seconds after the two of them sat down, Gladys began to present her case. "For the past three years we have moved more and more away from the main purpose of the church," she argued. "Bible study and prayer have been put on the back burner and social issues get all of our attention. If it is not one thing it is another. Sometimes I wonder if we have forgotten the gospel completely. Pastor, this is a sinful world and people need to hear God's word. Every time I open the paper I read something about drugs, theft, or sexual abuse. For too long we have tried to live on our own, doing what we think is right. How will we know what is right if we don't listen to God? How will we know what battles to fight if we don't read God's word?"

David often disagreed with the Women's Church Club president, but this time he thought she made valid points. He just listened and thanked her for coming in. She seemed surprised that David didn't argue. David was surprised things had gone so well.

There wasn't much time to sit around and be elated. David quickly turned to the work at hand, writing a sermon. Before he could get paper in the typewriter, there was a knock on the door and Trygvie walked in, gesturing and talking with such speed that whole paragraphs burst forth in a single breath. "Some people think that to be religious you either stand around with your hands folded all day long and your nose in the Bible or you walk down the street talking to the heathen about God. Well, there are a lot of hurting people out there, and if we are going to be on God's side we had better do more than talk and pray. We'd better roll up our sleeves and help them. We'd better be willing to go to work."

Again David did little but listen. Again he felt empathy for the speaker's position. And again he felt the pressure to finish the sermon for the next day.

On Sunday, several people pulled David aside to give their account of the past week's activities. During these conversations, he learned that some of the younger couples had met to discuss whether they should leave the church and that a number of older women were very upset.

On Sunday evening, Palmer Flugstad stopped by the house to tell David why he and Thelma hadn't been in church that morning. "Pastor," Palmer said slowly. "After talking with Gladys Olson, Thelma is so upset about the direction of our church that she just couldn't worship today. For the first time in years we stayed home. We kinda went to church though. We watched that smiley guy on TV."

After the children were in bed that evening, David and Doris talked. Finally Doris had a suggestion. "I think you ought to talk to Knute Lee. He knows this community better than anyone." Until his retirement last year, Knute had been a pastor in the community for twenty-five years. He had also been the substitute preacher the Sunday, Gladys and Trygvie started their squabble.

David quickly agreed. "I'll call him right now to see if he'll meet me tomorrow morning."

The appointment was made for 8:30 A.M. As David approached the café, he felt nervous. A conversation with Knute Lee—blunt, fearless Knute Lee—was always an adventure. David was never sure whether he would find his old friend compassionate and gentle or tough and cynical.

The old pastor was waiting for David and greeted him warmly, nearly crushing his hand with his iron grip. After a few seconds of chitchat, David got right to the point. "You are well aware of the squabble taking place at church," he said. "I've got two groups developing. They both have valid concerns, but neither is willing to listen to the other. Do you have any advice on how to deal with them?"

Knute looked skeptically at David for a moment before he spoke. "You and I evidently see the situation differently. You think they both have valid points. I think they are both off base. Remember, being half right is like walking on one leg."

Knute took a sip from the glass of orange juice in front of him. "For starters I am not impressed with the way either group views sin."

David looked baffled.

Knute assumed the role of the teacher. "Trygvie and his friends primarily see sin as social. Consequently, they focus on injustice and corporate greed. Gladys and her folks, on the other hand, see sin primarily as individual acts. They concentrate on sexual sins, and problems of honesty and personal morality."

David interrupted, "Sin can be either corporate or individual. That is why I think they both have valid points."

Knute raised his hand impatiently. "The issue is both groups are concerned with sins they don't have. Gladys isn't tempted to use heroin. I can't see her good friend Anita Disrud struggling with petty theft. The same goes for Trygvie. He has nothing to do with corporate investments and he is thousands of miles away from South Africa. Both of them fight the sins of others."

Knute leaned forward and spoke with intensity, in a near whisper. "I don't mean to suggest that people who are not troubled with child abuse shouldn't be alarmed with the effects of that evil. My point is this, people who truly hate sin hate their own sin. I will be much more impressed with both groups when they focus on their own backbiting, gossip, and anger."

Both men waited while the waitress refilled David's cup of coffee. Then Knute continued, "This whole problem is a theological one. First is the issue of sin, but second, is the issue of discipleship. Both groups have a partial view of what it means to love and follow God."

Knute thought for a moment. "Perhaps the best way to say this is to look at the gospel lessons for the next two weeks. Next Sunday is Trygvie's day, the story of the good Samaritan. It is followed with the story of Mary and Martha, Gladys's story. Each story is incomplete by itself. It needs the other to be fully understood. Actually the two stories illustrate the lawyer's summary of law: Love the Lord your God with all your heart, with all your soul, and with all your mind, and love your neighbor as yourself."

David joined in. "The parable of the good Samaritan teaches that true discipleship involves love for the person in need, the person who has been harmed by injustice. It affirms Trygvie's point."

"Ah," Knute said, "but that is only half the truth. We are also called to love the Lord our God with all our heart, soul, strength and mind. That is what Mary does when she sits at the Lord's feet. That phrase, 'to sit at the Lord's feet,' meant the same as to study under someone. In this case Mary is affirmed because she is attentive to the teaching of Jesus. To love the Lord with your whole being is to be submissive to Jesus and to learn from him."

"That is Gladys's point," David said.

"True," Knute countered, "but again it is still half the formula. Some want to sit at the feet of Jesus but avoid the feet of the injured. Others want to reach out to the world but never reach in to God. Both are needed."

"You know that a lot of people are troubled with the Mary and Martha story because it looks like a put down of the traditional feminine role," David said.

"Pigs' knuckles! This story is revolutionary in its support of women. Jesus lets the world know that women ought to be allowed to learn just like the men. In fact, he chides Martha for not spending time in reflection and prayer. This story is a warning that if we become activists without reflection, study or prayer, we miss God. Martha is distracted with too much serving, too much activity. It can happen to us as well. Both are needed."

David continued the thought: "We have got to read both stories together. They are really meant to supplement each other."

"Instead," Knute said, "people use them as mutually exclusive. They act as if it is either social action or prayer. If it is full discipleship, it must be both. People can't read a bit of Scripture and stop."

When David got home that morning, he had a brilliant idea. Why not invite both sides to join him for a two-week Bible study on the two texts? The first week they would study the good Samaritan, before it was preached, and the second week the Mary and Martha story. David spent most of Monday and Tuesday preparing and calling the parties involved.

Last Thursday was the second study. Was it a success? No. Despite what David thought was one of his best presentations, each group seemed to be more convinced than ever that they were right and the other was wrong. The last report was that they had made no progress.

The Homecoming

It was Friday night and James Allen Pike III was the last one out of the office. It was a tradition, started by his grandfather and continued by his father, to send the employees home early one weekend a month, and to close the shop himself. He made certain the coffee pots and other machines were turned off, that all the doors were locked, and that the bright blue outdoor sign that read, "PIKE'S PRINTING PLACE," was lit for the weekend.

Jim walked into his father's office to turn on the answering machine. For a moment he gazed around the spacious room. He looked at the pictures of famous politicians on the wall. Although semi-retirement for the elder Pike meant that the room was now used only periodically, it had been a seat of power for politics and religion during his father's long career. During the time James Pike had been chairman of one of the county's political parties, governors, senators, and even presidential candidates had arrived to pay homage to the man some called Boss Pike and to seek his support.

Many people believe that First Lutheran Church had also been run from that office. Jim shook his head and thought, "My father was, no make that *is*, a powerful figure."

Just the night before, leaders of the congregation had gathered quietly in that office to discuss the future of Pastor Dahl. The pastor had fallen out of favor with James Pike II, which was normally a prelude to a quick exit from First Lutheran. "The man's priorities are all mixed up," his father had bellowed. "He has forgotten the people who called him. He is neglecting shut-ins and the youth. He isn't even teaching a Bible class on Sunday mornings this fall."

Young Jim had left the meeting troubled and confused. He liked Chris Dahl, both as a pastor and a friend. Still, the charges against the pastor came from men who were old family friends. Now, nearly twenty-four hours later, Jim sat in one of his father's chairs and began to review the events of the previous evening.

Following the opening tirade, his father turned to Phil Bagley and said, "Phil, tell the group what you've observed."

"Well, you all know that Lorna and I walk most mornings about 7:30. For the past several weeks we've been stopping on the way back for a cup of coffee at Thelma's Diner. Its kind of a dive, but it is only three blocks from the house. Well, I don't have to tell you about some of the people who hang out at Thelma's in the morning. People like Pete Grayson and Andy Faucet. There's a whole table of them. Believe me, I'd count the silverware before that crew left. Anyway, the last couple weeks, who is sitting smack dab in the middle of the table, but Pastor Dahl."

Nearly every head in the room shook in silent disapproval.

Phil continued, "There's more. Hank, who practically lives next door to the Dahls can tell you stuff that will make your hair stand on end."

Hank moved forward in his seat to share his information. "I think we all know what happened last Thanksgiving. When the council turned down the pastor's request for a meal for the disadvantaged at church, he held it at his house, which isn't really his house. After all, it is a parsonage. The point is, it was Thanksgiving, a time for families to get together, and when the neighbors looked out their windows they saw this convoy of jalopies headed to the parsonage. The neighborhood looked like a junkyard. There were more rusty pickups than you can find at Severson's Salvage."

Hank continued, saying, "Now, I can understand people getting real generous once a year, specially on one of the family holidays, but last week wasn't Thanksgiving, and the same crew arrived again for some kind of outdoor meal. Maybe a wiener roast. All I know is that the neighborhood was full of welfare cheats and crooks. A couple of those folks have been caught shoplifting. I swear, he's making people nervous. It's a respectable neighborhood. You'd never think that a parsonage would lower property values."

James got back in the conversation. "How many of you in this room have ever been invited to the pastor's house for a meal?" A single hand was raised. "Just as I thought—only Jimmy. Leaders of the congregation aren't invited, but, to borrow Hank's phrase, 'welfare-cheats and crooks' have been. So, I ask you, who does this man work for?"

During that long meeting, Jim had asked only one question of his father: "Dad, do we know for certain that the youth and old people are being ignored?"

His father had glared at him. "It stands to reason that if Pastor Dahl is spending all of his time at Thelma's, something isn't getting done. We know he isn't teaching a Bible class this fall. He says there is no class because nobody comes. How is that for an excuse?"

There was more to sort through, but Jim could see by his watch that it was time to leave. It was about a seventy minute drive to Bass Lake Bible Camp, where he was attending a men's retreat. He had just enough time if he left immediately. A high school friend, Todd Warren, had invited him. It felt good to be going to a retreat where no one knew him or anything about First Lutheran. Besides, the theme for the weekend was, "The Homecoming." It sounded safe and comforting.

The retreat began with a nice meal. When they finished, the men were invited to bring their Bibles and to gather in a large room around a blazing fire. After each had introduced himself, Grady Wilson, the retreat speaker began. "During my three presentations we will study the 15th chapter of the Gospel of St. Luke. Tonight, I want to focus on the first ten verses. I hope to help you discover how these stories are your stories. Perhaps you will identify with one of the characters in the stories. Now, to start, will someone please read these ten verses out loud?"

A big man with a booming voice volunteered to read. His voice built to a dramatic climax when he finished the parable of the lost sheep: "And when he has found it he lays it on his shoulders, rejoicing. And when he comes home, he calls together his friends and his neighbors, saying to them, 'Rejoice with me, for I have found my sheep which was lost.' Just so, I tell you, there will be more joy in heaven over one sinner who repents than over ninety-nine righteous persons who need no repentance."

Eyes shifted from texts to the main speaker, who asked, "Can you think of any contemporary picture that is similar to this?"

The man who just read responded, "Scott O'Grady!"

"Interesting," the speaker said. "Explain why."

"Well, I thought of him first of all because he has the same name as you. I don't hear the name Grady that often. Of course, he was the guy the Serbs shot down. When that happened, our government did everything they could to find their lost sheep. They spared no cost. When they found him, the whole country rejoiced. Parties and parades broke out all over the place."

"Excellent," the speaker said, nodding. "God is like those who search for a lost pilot. He will go anywhere, at any cost, to find that lost person. God has a passion for the lost. God will not rest until those who are lost have been found. What a wonderful insight!"

He then looked over the group. "What kind of lost persons was Jesus talking about?" Like many questions asked by a Bible study leader, this one was greeted with total silence. Finally he decided to give them a hint. "Look at the first verses of the chapter."

Bibles opened and eyes searched for the key words. Todd was the first to speak, saying, "Tax collectors and sinners, whoever they were."

Grady responded, "Tax collectors and sinners were people who were not acceptable in polite society. They were people with bad reputations. Tax collectors were Jews who collected taxes for a foreign government, and kept plenty for themselves. Sinners were people who were guilty of scandalous behavior. If the sinner was a woman, she may have been a whore. The man could have been someone who had committed a crime or made his living on the edge of the law."

Jim was puzzled and asked, "You said we are to identify with someone in the story. Are we suppose to be on the side of Jesus, or are we suppose to read the story like one of his critics?"

"You have summarized our two choices," Grady said with a smile. "First, we can listen like critics. We can say, 'What in the world is Jesus doing with all those slimy people?' We can ask how appropriate it is to hang out with folks who are unscrupulous. Like they say, "Birds of a feather flock together." We can question the approach of Jesus."

Grady collected his thoughts before he continued. "Or we can identify with Jesus, who shared God's passion for the poor and the lost. We can tell the world, If you enjoy bashing the poor, you will find yourself on the opposite side of Jesus. Jesus was a friend and supporter of the have-nots. He never romanticized them. He knew they could be cranky and mean like the rest of us. But, Jesus treated them like he treats everyone, as children of God."

Grady brought his words to a close, "The good news is, there is a great celebration in heaven when one lost person returns. Jesus says,

'Do you want to get in on the party? Do you want to share the joy? Then, work with those the rest of society rejects.'"

There was silence in the room until Todd broke in, "Isn't there a third alternative? I'm not so vain as to identify with Jesus. I'm not going to say, 'It's you and me against the world, Jesus.' Nor am I a critic. I may not share in everything he has done, but neither do I criticize him for spending time with any particular group of people."

"So," Jim asked his friend, "what is the third alternative?"

"I'm just one of those who find myself welcomed and forgiven in the presence of God, who comes to God for a bit of his grace and mercy. I guess the third alternative is to identify with the sinners."

As Jim drove his car back home on Sunday afternoon, his head was spinning. It had been an exciting weekend. The Friday night session led to a discussion that ranged far into the morning. The presentations and discussions the next day were equally stimulating.

After the comfort of the retreat, coming home felt like entering a hostile environment. It also meant that he needed a face-to-face discussion with the elder James Pike. The retreat gave him the courage he needed to confront his father.

Jim rehearsed his homecoming speech. "Dad, for the first time in my life, I must disagree with you. You are wrong, dead wrong about Pastor Dahl. You've criticized him for eating with people you find undesirable. Dad, you sound just like the critics of Jesus. You ask who Pastor Dahl works for. Well, he doesn't just work for the council at First Lutheran. He can't let any group of people write his sermons, tell him how to pray, or what to say to someone who is dying. Nor can they tell him he can't eat with certain people. He works for Jesus, and Jesus himself spent time, lots of time, with people like the ones you find at Thelma's. How dare any of us criticize the pastor for inviting poor people into his home? Rather than reprimand him, we ought to first thank him and then imitate him."

He gave the speech several times during the drive home. Each time it got better, and he became more bold. "By golly," he thought, "I'm going to drive over to see Dad tonight. I need to get this off my chest."

Jim drove into town, turned down the street where his father lived, and stopped four doors away. There he sat for nearly five minutes thinking about an argument with James Pike II. Finally he sighed, started the engine, and drove past his father's house toward his own home. "Maybe," he thought, "it would be better if we talk tomorrow."

Greedy Sons

The Sufi Masters, a group of mystic Muslims in Persian, Arabic, and Turkish cultures, taught through story. This story is adapted from one of their tales.

There was once a hard-working and generous farmer who had several idle and greedy sons. On his deathbed, he told them that they would find his treasure if they were to dig in a certain field. As soon as the old man was dead, the sons hurried to the field and proceeded to dig it up from one end to another in search of the treasure. The longer they worked, the more desperate they became. Yet, they did not find a single ounce of gold.

Surveying the field, they reasoned that in his generosity their father must have given his gold away during his lifetime. Just as they abandoned their search, it occurred to them that since the land had been prepared they might as well sow a crop. They planted wheat, which produced an abundant yield. When it matured they sold their crop and prospered.

After the harvest was in, the sons thought again about the rare possibility that they might have missed the buried gold. Once again they dug up their fields, with the same result.

After several years they became accustomed to labor and to the cycle of the seasons, something which they had not understood before. Finally they understood that their father had been training them to become hard-working farmers. As time passed they became wealthy through the work of their hands and no longer wondered about the hidden hoard.

Master *and* Servant

Based on a Sufi story, this tale reminds us of the similarities between the teachings of Jesus and the instruction of Mohammed.

A young man came to the Teacher asking if he might be his disciple. "You are not ready," the Teacher replied kindly. But when the young man persisted, the Teacher relented.

"I am going on a trip," the Teacher said. "You may accompany me."

The young man was overjoyed.

"When the journey is completed, you will answer this question: 'Who is greater, a master or his servant?' On the journey there are two roles," the Teacher said. "One must lead and the other must follow. Which role do you prefer?"

"It is only appropriate that you be the leader," the man said.

On the first night, as the two men prepared their meal over a fire, it began to rain. The Teacher got up and held a covering over the disciple to protect him. "But that is what I should do for you," the man said.

"I command you to allow me to protect you," said the Teacher. And the man did.

The next day the young man said, "Today let me be the leader and you follow me." The Teacher agreed.

"I will collect wood to make a fire," the man said.

"You will do no such a thing," the Teacher said. "I shall collect it."

"I command you to sit as I collect the wood," the young man said.

"You may do no such thing," said the Teacher. "It is not proper for a master to serve his disciple."

And so it went every day. No matter which role he accepted, the Teacher ran errands and performed services for the young man. At the end of the journey, the Teacher drew the young man aside. "Are you ready with an answer to my question?" he asked.

"I am a bit confused," the young man said. "In most cases the master is greater, but with you things are unclear."

"Your confusion is healthy," the Teacher concluded. "In society the one who sits at table is greater than the one who waits on table. It is not so in the kingdom. In the kingdom the greatest is the one who provides caring service."

The Teacher's Advice

Vengeance belongs to God alone. This teaching of Jesus is echoed in this folktale, which I adapted from an Italian source.

There was a shopkeeper who was caught cheating. Since it was his first offense, the judge did not send him to jail. Convinced that he would always wear the stigma of a crook in his hometown, the shopkeeper decided to leave home and start a new life. Before departing, the shopkeeper put all of his money in an envelope and left it, along with a note, for his wife. The note read: "I know I have humiliated you and our three young sons. The money in this envelope ought to be enough to take care of you until I can gain self-respect and return."

After leaving, the shopkeeper wandered for several days. Then one night he saw a group of people gathered around a tall man with a long beard. They listened intently while the bearded man spoke to them. When it was over, and the crowd began to drift away, the Teacher, as he was known, walked over to the man and spoke. "If you need a place to stay tonight, you are welcome to sleep in my guest room."

What began as overnight accommodations stretched into months and years. The former shopkeeper worked for the Teacher, and in return received room, board, and a few coins each week. After years passed, the former shopkeeper approached his friend and said, "I am grateful that you allowed me to start life over again. Now it is time to return home."

The Teacher nodded and asked him to come into his study, where the Teacher counted out 300 gold coins. "I have kept track of the money I owe you. It ought to be enough to start life over again with your family."

The man thanked the Teacher, and headed for the door. "Many people come to you for advice," the man said before leaving. "How much do you charge?"

"One hundred gold coins."

The man thought for a moment, and handed back one-third of his gold. "Give me a word of advice."

"Do not abandon the old road for the new," the Teacher said.

The former shopkeeper thought that the advice was very expensive, but over the years he had seen how others profited from the words of the Teacher. As he reached the porch, he handed the Teacher an additional 100 gold coins. "Give me another word of advice."

"Don't meddle in other people's business," the Teacher said.

"I now have only 100 gold coins," the man thought to himself. "I came with nothing, I might as well return with nothing." He handed the Teacher the rest of his money. "I'd like another word of advice."

"Put off anger until tomorrow."

Now it was time to go. As the man was about to leave the property, the Teacher shouted, "Here is a special loaf of bread for your homecoming. Do not eat it until you are with your entire family."

The man walked for several miles before he fell in with three other men who were headed in the same direction. When they came to a fork in the road, the three men went to the right. "It is a new short cut," they told the former shopkeeper.

Remembering the advice of the Teacher, he chose to stay on the old road. A few minutes later he heard gunfire and shouts. The other travelers were being attacked by bandits. When the shooting ceased, he stopped and gave thanks for his old friend's advice, which had saved his life.

Later he met two other travelers and walked with them until they reached an inn. As they were paying their bill, an argument broke out between his two companions and the innkeeper. The companions claimed the food was bad and refused to pay. All three men turned to the former shopkeeper to settle the dispute. Remembering the second piece of advice of the Teacher, he refused to get involved, paid his bill, and went to his room.

Up in his room he listened as the argument broke into a fight. Soon the authorities arrived and arrested the two dinner companions, taking them to jail. Once again the man gave thanks for good advice.

He walked two more days before he came to the town he left years earlier. He found his old neighborhood and gazed at his old house from across the street. After a few minutes his wife walked by the window, holding the hand of a handsome youth. The sight made the man so angry that he reached for his gun. Before he acted, however, he remembered the third piece of advice from the Teacher: "Put off anger until tomorrow."

The man calmed down enough to ask a woman walking down the street if she knew who lived in his old house. "A very happy woman," came the reply. "Her oldest son just returned from seminary, where he is studying to become a pastor. I believe she is having a party in his honor tomorrow."

In joy, the man ran across the street and introduced himself to his wife and sons. His homecoming made the party that was planned an even greater celebration. When everyone had left, the man asked the family to gather around the table where he cut open the loaf of bread given him by the Teacher. Inside he found 300 gold coins, which the Teacher had taken so that his advice would be valued.

The Peacemaker

The continent of Africa is a rich source of stories for our gatherings.

A large terrier was upset as he watched two other dogs fight each other. "Fighting makes no sense," he said to himself. "I will make them stop." Quickly, he ran between the two snarling animals, pushing the bigger of the two aside. To his great surprise, the other dog turned on him and began to attack him. Soon the large dog joined in until the peacemaker was battered and bruised.

The Happy Man's Shirt

This story, which has become a favorite of many American
storytellers, can be found in the folk literature of many cultures.

The queen could not understand why the prince was so unhappy. "My son has everything any young man could ever want," she said to the king. "He is handsome, intelligent, and very rich."

"Yes," the king replied, "but he remains very unhappy."

Musicians, jugglers, clowns, and actors were invited to the palace to entertain the royal family. The prince politely watched each performer, on occasion smiled, and always applauded at the end of every act. But when they left he was still unhappy.

In vain his father attempted to interest him in hunting and other sport. In vain his mother attempted to interest him in painting or writing poetry, but no matter what the prince did, he remained unhappy. Finally the queen invited a wise and kind woman to visit the palace. "Live with our family for several weeks," the queen said. "Observe my son, and if need be, engage him in quiet conversation. Perhaps you can offer him a way out of the darkness."

After several weeks the wise woman invited the entire royal family to gather with her in the chamber room. "Most of the people in the kingdom believe you live an ideal life," the woman began. "They envy your good looks, your intelligence, and most of all, your wealth. Your son, however, seems to be saddened by his good fortune. Above everything else, his wealth appears to make him unhappy."

"What solution do you offer?" the king asked anxiously.

"My advice," the woman said softly, "is to send the prince on a journey to seek a genuinely happy man. When your son finds him, he should exchange shirts with the happy man."

The prince accepted the suggestion of the wise woman and left immediately in search of a happy man. During the next three months, the prince interviewed men who were rich and others who were poor. He interviewed men who were married and those who were single. Not one man he interviewed met his criteria of a genuinely happy man.

Then one day as he traveled down a winding road, the prince heard a man singing at the top of his lungs from behind a wall. "Hello there," the prince cried out.

The prince heard a noise on the other side of the wall, and soon he saw a man peering over the top. "Sorry I can't be more polite," the man said with a twinkle in his eye, "but I had to stand on a rock to see you."

"Why were you singing?" the prince asked.

"Because I love to sing," the man said. "Of course I also love to work, dance, and read. I guess I love to do almost everything. I'm a very contented man."

"I'd like you to come back with me and live in our palace," the prince said.

"Thank you for your offer," the man smiled, "but I prefer to stay right here. I wouldn't trade my wonderful life with any king in the world."

"If you won't come back with me, I ask just one favor," the prince said. "Change shirts with me."

"That's not possible," the man said pulling himself up to the top of the wall.

When he looked the prince understood. The happy man wore no shirt.

It Could Always Be Worse

This Yiddish folktale uses hyperbole and humor to make a serious point.

A poor devout woman lived with her husband, their five children, and her mother in a one-room hut. The children were noisy, and the crowded conditions often produced loud arguments. In summer, when the family spent many hours outdoors, life was bearable, but when winter arrived the family felt trapped because the small house was filled with crying and quarreling. One day when the woman couldn't stand it anymore, she ran to the Teacher for advice.

"Teacher," she cried, "life is miserable. My husband, our five children, my mother, and I are so crowded in our little hut that we argue and quarrel every day. I can't stand the noise anymore. Please help me. I'll do whatever you say."

The Teacher pondered her request for several minutes. Then he asked, "Do you have any chickens?"

"Certainly," the woman replied. "We have six chickens, a rooster, and a goose."

"Excellent," said the Teacher. "Go home and bring the chickens, the rooster, and the goose into your hut to live with you."

The woman was surprised, but she immediately left for home, promising to move the poultry into the house.

After a week passed, the woman returned to the Teacher. "Life is worse than before," she told the teacher. "In addition to crying and quarreling, we now have honking, crowing, and clucking. Yesterday we all had feathers in our soup. The hut seems smaller and the children seem larger. Please help me!"

The Teacher considered the woman's words before he spoke. "Do you have a goat?" he asked.

"Yes," she said slowly. "We have an old goat, tied to a pole behind our house."

"Excellent," said the Teacher. "Untie the goat and let it live in your hut with you."

"Teacher, we are already crowded," the woman cried.

"You did ask for my help, didn't you?" the Teacher responded.

The poor woman walked home, untied the goat, and brought it in the hut. Five days later she returned. "Teacher," she said desperately, "everything is worse. Now, in addition to the crying, quarreling, honking, crowing, and clucking, we have a goat pushing and butting everyone with his horns. The hut seems even smaller."

The Teacher asked, "Do you have a cow?"

"Yes," the woman said fearfully, "we have a cow."

"Go home and take the cow into your hut."

"Oh, no, Teacher," the woman cried. "My family will be angry."

"Tell them the Teacher has ordered it."

The poor woman went home and told her husband to move the cow into the hut.

"Is the Teacher crazy?" he shouted.

Still, they moved the cow into the hut.

Three days later the woman returned. "Life is a nightmare," the woman cried. "Now, in addition to the crying, quarreling, honking, crowing, clucking, and butting, the cow tramples everything. We all argue and shout at one another. Help me, please!"

The Teacher smiled. "Go home and let the animals out of your hut."

The woman turned and went home as fast as she could run. As she ran she yelled, "Thank you, Teacher, thank you."

As soon as she reached home the woman, and her husband let the cow, the goat, the chickens, the goose, and the rooster out of their hut.

That night the poor man and all his family slept peacefully. There was no honking, crowing, clucking, butting, or trampling. There was also no arguing or fighting.

The very next morning the woman and her husband came to the Teacher. "We wish to thank you for your help," the man said.

"Life is sweet and peaceful," the woman responded. "We love our home. It is quiet, peaceful, and so roomy."

The Dirty Piece *of* Pastry

This story is adapted from a Jewish folktale.

A wealthy businessman decided to take a walk and eat his lunch at the same time. As he strolled near a large park, he purchased a hot dog and a soft drink. On two occasions, men approached him and asked, "Can you help me. I'm hungry?" Each time the businessman looked straight ahead and kept walking.

Later, for dessert, he bought a chocolate éclair from a vendor. Just as he was about to take his first bite of the pastry, he had to jump out of the way to avoid a young boy on a skateboard. The éclair fell to the ground, landing in a wet area. The businessman picked it up and tried to clean it, but it was useless. The pastry was caked with mud.

As he was about to throw the éclair away, an idea struck him. He walked over to one of the beggars and handed him the dirty pastry. "Here, my good man, is something for your hunger." He smiled to himself, and walked back to his office.

That night the businessman dreamed he was sitting in a large, crowded café with waitresses running back and forth, bringing customers delicious cakes and tortes. The waitresses all ignored the businessman, though he waved at them continually. Finally he caught the eye of a young woman and asked for something to eat. She returned in a few minutes with a dirty piece of pastry.

The man was outraged. "You can't treat me this way," he insisted. "I have the right to be served like anyone else. I expect to get good value for my money."

"You don't seem to understand," the waitress said kindly. "You can't buy anything here. We don't accept money. You have just arrived in heaven, and all you can order here is what you sent ahead while you were on earth. The only item we have listed in your name is this muddy éclair."

Taking It With You

This story comes from the
Reverend Warren Keating of Derby, Kansas.

Once there was a very rich man who bombarded the throne of God with petitions, asking for the right to take his wealth with him when he died. Each time the man made his request, God replied, "There is no need to take it with you."

Finally, however, God decided to relent. "Since you refuse to listen to me, I will allow you to take a portion of what you have with you. You may take as much as you can carry in a suitcase."

The man was ecstatic and immediately purchased the largest steamer trunk he could find. He then set upon the task of determining what portion of his estate he would place in the trunk. "If I take stocks or bonds," he reasoned, "it may be impossible to redeem them. If I take currency, it is not clear whether I should bring dollars, pounds, francs, or marks."

Finally he decided to bring gold. "There is always a market for gold," he thought. Quickly, he turned most of his wealth into gold bullion and placed the heavy bricks into his trunk. Then he put the trunk next to his bed, and waited to die.

After the rich man died, he showed up at the gates of heaven carrying his trunk. St. Peter said, "Sorry. People who enter these gates must come empty-handed."

"I have special permission," the man insisted.

St. Peter looked in the record book and was amazed. "I've never seen this allowed before. Do you mind if I look in your trunk?"

"Not at all," the man said, as he proudly opened the large container that had been packed with gleaming bricks of bullion.

St. Peter carefully examined the contents of the trunk and then looked befuddled at the rich man. "Paving stones," he said shaking his head. "Why did you decide to bring paving stones?"

The Honest Neighbor

This is a Jewish folktale.

In a large city lived two merchants—one Jewish and one Christian—both bought and sold jewels. They were competitors as well as friends. One day the king sent out a decree banishing all Jews from the land. He gave them only two days before they had to leave.

The Jewish merchant cried out to his Christian friend, "It will be impossible for me to transport all of my jewels. Since I don't know where I will find a new home, I can't be certain that they will be safe. What should I do?"

"Leave them in my care," the Christian merchant said. "This ban will soon pass and then you will be allowed back in the land. I give you my solemn promise before God that I will keep all your jewels safe until you return."

Greatly relieved, the Jewish merchant gave his entire stock to his friend before fleeing the city.

Many years passed before the king died. The first edict of his son, the new king, was to welcome Jews back into the city. The Jewish merchant had neither spoken or written to his friend since his exile. He returned to the city not knowing what to expect. Was his friend still alive? Had he kept his word and saved the jewels?

Everything looked strange to the Jewish merchant as he wandered back into the city he once called home. He approached his old neighborhood with trepidation and then looked in terror when he saw his friend's shop. What had once been a proud business in a prosperous neighborhood now stood in ruins. The shop was boarded up, and his house that stood next to it was in total disrepair.

"I have lost everything!" he cried out loud. "My business is gone and my friend is no more."

Then, out of the shambles came an old man. It was the Christian merchant. "Shortly after you left," he explained, "my shop went up in flames. I lost nearly everything. I have lived in poverty ever since."

"Why didn't you use my jewels to start over?" the Jewish merchant cried. "You had them in your possession."

"I was not afraid of losing my wealth," the friend replied, "but I did not want to lose my honesty. I made a sacred promise that I would care for your jewels, and I have kept it. All that you left in my care can be found in the cellar."

Before the week was over, the Jewish merchant reopened his shop. He shared his wealth with his honest neighbor, and the Jew and Christian lived as brothers to the ends of their lives.

The Church Lady

This story is adapted from an Irish folktale.

There once was a woman who had the reputation of being very holy. She never missed a worship service. She not only attended church every Sunday morning, but also every midweek worship and special seasonal services.

One day a friend said to her, "How many times a year do you attend worship? I would think the number is close to one hundred."

Intrigued with the question, the woman decided to keep track. She built a wooden box, locked it, and hid the key where no one could find it. Each time she returned home from worship, she placed a pebble in the box. Whenever she came home from church, she never forgot to put a pebble in the box.

As the years passed, the woman began to wonder if the box was getting too heavy to lift. She asked a strong man who lived in her town to help her carry the box outside. "Be careful," she said. "It is very heavy."

The strong man picked up the box effortlessly and said, "Your box is very light. I don't think you'll need my help in moving it."

Quickly, the woman found her key and opened the box. She looked inside and found only five stones. She stood speechless, gazing into the almost empty box.

After some time, the woman walked to church and told her pastor the story. "It doesn't seem possible that someone has stolen the pebbles out of my box," she said. "It was locked, secured, and the key was hidden."

The wise pastor spoke kindly to the woman. "Your box tells us that when you attended worship, God has not been central in your mind and your neighbors have not been central in your prayers. It is clear that most of the time you were thinking about how pious and holy you were, and how everyone ought to know how devoted you have been to the church. This is a sign from heaven that only five times have you entered worship with a heart turned to God. True worship does not consist in the number of times we enter a building."

The Creation

This poem, published by James Weldon Johnson in 1927, is a terrific example of storytelling through preaching.

And God stepped out on space,
And He looked around and said: I'm lonely—
I'll make me a world.
And far as the eye of God could see
Darkness covered everything,
Blacker than a hundred midnights
Down in a cypress swamp.
Then God smiled,
And the light broke,
And the darkness rolled up on one side,
And the light stood shining on the other,
And God said: That's good!
Then God reached out and took the light in His hands,
And God rolled the light around in His hands
Until He made the sun;
And He set that sun a-blazing in the heavens.
And the light that was left from making the sun
God gathered it up in a shining ball
And flung it against the darkness,

Spangling the night with the moon and stars.
Then down between
The darkness and the light
He hurled the world;
And God said: That's good!
Then God himself stepped down—
And the sun was on His right hand,
And the moon was on His left;
The stars were clustered about His head,
And the earth was under His feet.
And God walked, and where He trod
His footsteps hollowed the valleys out
And bulged the mountains up.
Then He stopped and looked and saw
That the earth was hot and barren.
So God stepped over the edge of the world
And He spat out the seven seas—
He batted His eyes, and the lightning flashed—
He clapped His hands, and the thunders rolled—
And the waters above the earth came down,
The cooling waters came down.
Then the green grass sprouted,
And the little red flowers blossomed,
The pine tree pointed His finger to the sky,
And the oak spread out His arms,
The lakes cuddled down in the hollows of the ground,
And the rivers ran down to the sea;
And God smiled again,
And the rainbow appeared,
And curled itself around His shoulder.
Then God raised His arm and He waved His hand
Over the sea and over the land,
And He said: Bring forth! Bring forth!
And quicker than God could drop His hand,
Fishes and fowls
And beasts and birds

Swam the rivers and the seas,
Roamed the forests and the woods,
And split the air with their wings.
And God said, That's good!
Then God walked around,
And God looked around
On all that He had made.
He looked at His sun,
And He looked at His moon,
And He looked at His little stars;
And He looked on His world
With all its living things,
And God said, I'm lonely still.
Then God sat down—
On the side of a hill where He could think;
By a deep, wide river He sat down;
With His head in His hands.
God thought and thought,
Til He thought: I'll make me a man!
Up from the bed of river God scooped the clay;
And by the bank of the river
He knelt Him down;
And there the great God Almighty
Who lit the sun and fixed it in the sky,
Who flung the stars to the most far corner of the night,
Who rounded the earth in the middle of His hand;
This Great God,
Like a mammy bending over her baby,
Kneeled down in the dust
Toiling over a lump of clay
Til He shaped it in His own image;
Then into it He blew the breath of life,
And man became a living soul.
Amen.
Amen.

CHAPTER IV

Wisdom
and
Foolishness

The Astronomer

A *fable of Aesop.*

Each night an astronomer went out to observe the stars. One evening, as he wandered on the edge of a city, the astronomer fell into a well. A neighbor heard his loud shouts of anguish and rushed to his rescue. The neighbor discovered the astronomer bruised and sore.

"Why do such terrible things happen to me?" the astronomer asked.

"Good friend," the neighbor replied, "rather than placing all your attention on the mysteries of heaven, perhaps you ought to pay a little attention to things here on earth."

The Deer *at the* Pool

A *fable of Aesop.*

One hot summer day a deer came to a pool to quench his thirst. As he stood there drinking, he saw his reflection in the water. "What beauty and strength are in these horns," he said, "but how weak and fragile are my feet." While the deer stood observing himself, a lion appeared nearby and crouched to spring upon him. The deer immediately took to flight. As long as the road was smooth, the deer easily out-distanced the lion. But upon entering the woods, the deer became entangled by his horns and the lion quickly caught him.

Facing the lion, the deer thought to himself, "What a fool I have been. The feet which almost saved me, I despised, while the antlers which I loved proved to be my destruction."

The Lion *and* His Councilors

A *fable of Aesop.*

A lion, a fox, and a donkey became partners and successfully acquired a large amount of food. The lion asked the donkey to divide the prize. Carefully, the donkey divided the spoil into three equal shares. The lion was offended, burst into a rage, and devoured the donkey.

Then the lion asked the fox to make a division. The fox accumulated all they had killed into one large heap and left but a small morsel for himself. The lion said, "This is perfect. Who taught you how to divide so well?"

The fox replied, "I just recently learned it from the donkey."

Wise people learn from the misfortunes of others.

The Girl *and the* Nettles

A fable of Aesop.

A girl was stung by a nettle. She ran home and cried to her mother, saying, "Even though I only touched it gently, it hurts very badly."

"That is why it stung you," said her mother. "The next time you touch a nettle, grasp it tightly, and it will not hurt you."

Whatever you do, do it boldly.

The Mouse *under the* Granary

A *fable of Leo Tolstoy.*

A mouse lived under a granary. She always had plenty to eat because there was a little hole in the granary floor that allowed grain to slip through and form a little pile each day.

The mouse was very proud of her situation and wanted to tell other mice how well she lived. She gnawed a larger hole to allow more grain to fall. Then she invited her friends for a feast.

When the friends arrived she discovered she had no grain, for the farmer had noticed the big hole and closed it up.

Friendship

This is a story by nineteenth-century Russian writer Ivan Kriloff.

Two dogs, Brownie and Big Red, had just finished eating and decided to lay in the shade to take a nap. "I have no finer friend than you," Brownie said to his companion. "How fortunate I am to be able to run and sleep with someone like you."

"I agree," Red Dog said, as he scratched himself. "Others argue and fight. But you and I are content just to have each other."

The two continued to speak of the joys of friendship until a cook opened the back door and threw a bone onto the grass. The two friends then leaped to their feet and raced to the bone. Each claimed the fragment for himself, and soon a fight broke out between the two dogs.

Money, like bones, often causes friendships to go the the dogs.

The Dog *in the* Mountains

An African fable.

Two mountains were separated by a valley. On the top of each mountain was a castle. Down in the valley a dog lay under a tree. Suddenly a trumpet blew from one of the castles signaling that supper was about to be served, the dog immediately ran up the mountain, hoping to find some tasty morsels to eat. When the dog had gone halfway up the mountain, however, he heard a trumpet blow from the other castle. The dog stopped, and hearing no trumpet from the mountain he was climbing, ran down the mountain and up toward the other castle. Halfway up that mountain he heard another series of blasts from the horn on the first mountain. Once again the dog changed his course and headed for his original destination.

He kept changing mountains until both horns were silent and the meals were over. Alas, the dog received no scraps from either castle.

The Peg

This story is adapted from a Jewish folktale.

There once was a beautiful princess who was besieged by young men who wanted to marry her. She consulted with her parents to determine a way to decide which man to marry. The queen advised her to select a man who made her heart sing, and the king advised her to select a man who was very wise. The princess decided to do both.

For several months she met individually with all of the young men who sought her hand in marriage. The princess discovered that there were only three who charmed her. She called the three together and said, "Tomorrow morning I want each of you to bring a handmade peg. I will marry the one who has made the finest peg."

The next morning all three men appeared at the appointed hour. The first produced a large peg that was bright and polished. The second gave the princess a smaller peg that was made of the finest wood. She then turned to the third man. "Where is your peg?"

"I didn't make a peg, Your Highness."

"And why not?"

"Because to make a peg you first must see the hole."

The princess smiled and accepted the hand of the third young man.

The Bishop's Wife

The riddle story is a favorite genre in folk literature.
Frequently a bishop, landowner, or an entire group of people
is challenged to answer a series of questions. Someone else, often
a wife or a servant, meets the challenge for them. This riddle
story is adapted from Irish and Jewish folktales.

When an old king died, his son began to rule the land. After only two months the son decided to review all of his father's appointments. He interviewed the royal secretary, the royal treasurer, and the viceroy. He found each unworthy and sent them in exile with only the clothes on their backs.

Next, the son decided to interview the local bishop to see if he was wise enough to retain his appointment. He sent a courier to the home of the bishop with this message:

> *You are to come to my office in*
> *three days to answer three questions:*
>
> *1. Which direction does God face?*
> *2. What is my worth?*
> *3. What am I thinking?*
>
> *If you fail to answer all questions correctly,*
> *you will be banished from my kingdom.*

The bishop studied the questions and threw up his hands in despair. "It is no use," he told his wife. "I have no idea how to answer the questions. I will be a beggar in my old age."

"I will go before the king in your place," his wife said calmly. "I have always been good at riddles."

"He will know immediately that you are not me," the husband protested.

"He has never met you," his wife explained. "If I dress in your clothes, cover myself with your cloak and your hood, and lower my voice, he will never suspect."

The bishop, who knew he would never know the answers, was desperate enough to allow his wife to try. As she strolled out of the house, he had to admit that she looked very much like a bishop.

When the bishop's wife arrived at the palace, she was brought before the king. "Let's begin immediately," the king said brusquely. "Which direction does God face?"

The bishop's wife walked over to a table where a candle was lit. "I have a question for you," she said. "In what direction does this candle give light?"

"You can see for yourself that it gives light in all directions," the king replied.

"Likewise God," the woman said. "For God's glory fills all creation."

"Well said," the king exclaimed. "Now for the second question. What is my worth?"

"Twenty-nine pieces of silver," the woman answered quickly.

The king laughed. "What a foolish answer," he exclaimed. "I have houses full of gold and silver. I have a kingdom with fertile fields and vineyards, and you say I am worth twenty-nine pieces of silver?"

"The gospels tell us," the bishop's wife said politely, "that our Lord Jesus Christ was sold for thirty pieces of silver. Surely you are not worth more than our Lord. Since you serve as Christ's regent in this land, I subtracted one silver coin to gauge your worth."

The king was amazed with the answer and accepted it. "I have one more question," he said. "What am I thinking?"

"Your majesty, you are thinking that I am the bishop," his wife said in her deepest voice. "But in fact I am not the bishop. I am his wife." Immediately she took off the hood and let her hair roll down to her shoulders.

The king looked shocked for a moment before he began to laugh. "You are indeed a wise woman. You have succeeded not only in answering my riddle but in fooling me with one of your own. Go home and tell your husband that he will remain bishop. Then come back to the palace and talk with me about a position in my government. We can use a person with your intelligence around here."

Patience

Several people have mailed different versions of this story to me.
Though the source is unclear, it appears to have a European origin.

For years a man had struggled to make a living. Then, learning how to bend fine timber slowly, he developed a business making wooden arches for carriage shafts. After several years, it appeared that he was on his way to becoming a wealthy man.

The wealthy man's neighbor became envious of the man's success and determined that since he had access to the same lumber, he would begin his own business. The neighbor's goal was to make twice as many shafts as the wealthy man. Quickly the neighbor cut trees and attempted to form them into shafts, but one after another split.

Finally the neighbor went to the wealthy man to ask for advice. "I use the same trees and I have similar equipment. Why am I unsuccessful?" he asked.

"You have both skill and fine materials," the wealthy man told his neighbor. "It takes a long time to bend the tree. What you lack is patience."

Sign Language

This humorous story can be found in many forms within the Jewish storytelling tradition.

A king was urged by his council of advisers to rid the country of all Jews. "They are a dishonest people," a senior adviser said. "They are not good members of the community. They stick to themselves, and they are not to be trusted."

"And yet," said the king, "they are highly intelligent."

"I don't wish to disagree," a second adviser said, "but I believe they are wise in a limited way. They know little about the real world." The king, who loved the art of sign disputation, decided to issue a challenge. "We will hold a contest between the wisest person among my advisers and the wisest person among the Jews. Whoever loses will be forced to leave the country."

The contest was set for two weeks from that day. When members of the Jewish community heard about the challenge, they cried out in anguish. No one wanted to carry the fate of the entire community on their shoulders. As the leaders were ringing their hands, a Jewish farmer came in front of the community. "What is the matter with you?" he asked. "You all look terrible."

They told him of the challenge set forth by the king, explaining that they couldn't find an opponent for the wisest of the king's advisers. "I'm your man," the farmer said confidently. "I'll match wits with anyone from the king's court." Since the farmer was the only one willing to meet in sign disputation, the community accepted his offer.

When the day of the contest arrived, the two opponents met in a large open area surrounded by large crowds. The king pointed to his adviser to begin.

The king's adviser pointed his arm toward the farmer, with two fingers spread apart. The farmer quickly raised his arm, with one finger in front of his face.

Finally the adviser reached into his pocket and took out a piece of cheese. The farmer reached into his pocket and pulled out an egg.

At this, the king's adviser dropped his head, shoot the farmer's hand, and walked away in defeat. Meanwhile, the crowd of Jewish people began a wild celebration.

When the other members of the king's court rallied around the adviser, he explained what happened. "I raised my arms toward the sky extending my fingers, declaring that our king has the power to scatter the farmer and his people all over the earth. He countered by raising a single fist, declaring that God would hold them together."

"Next," the adviser said, "I held up two fingers to tell him there are two kings—one in heaven and one on earth. He raised one finger, declaring that one king rules over all."

"Finally," the adviser continued, "I brought out a piece of cheese to say that all religion is growing old and moldy. But he brought out an egg to say it is still fresh and whole. He was a noble and wise opponent, and to think he was a mere farmer."

The Jewish people gathered around their new hero asking for an explanation of what had happened. "It is quite simple," he declared. "Before I knew the contest had started, he raised up both arms threatening to knock me over. I shook my fist in his face to say, 'If you do, I'll fight back.'"

"Then," went on the farmer, "the king's adviser spread out his fingers to poke me in both my eyes, and I countered by threatening to poke him in his eyes. By then he must have given up. He took out his lunch, so I took, out mine."

The king, who had watched the contest and had his own explanation of the outcome, sent all of his advisers out of the country and replaced them with a council of farmers.

God's Stupid Creatures

A fable from Cameroon

One day a spider and a millipede were discussing the advantages of not being human. "Human beings have the poorest hearing in all of God's creation," the millipede said. "When I stamp all my feet they don't hear a thing."

"They are also blind," the spider replied. "After I spin a splendid palace for myself, invariably some human will blunder along and destroy it."

"Their bodies must be ugly," the millipede added, "for they cover them up and don't allow anyone to see them as they were created by God."

"One more thing," the spider said quietly, "they don't' appreciate creation. They wear silly hats when the sun shines, and big umbrellas when the Creator sends the rain."

"What strange animals," the millipede concluded. "They seem to be too stupid to appreciate the gifts God has given them."

The Nightingale *and the* Donkey

A fable from East Africa.

A donkey, wandering down an old road to listen to a nightingale sing from the branch of a tree. When the nightingale saw that she had an audience, she gave her finest performance. "My voice has never sounded better," she said to herself.

"You do have a nice voice," the donkey shouted, "but where I come from we have a rooster who grows every morning. He can sing a lot louder than you can. You ought to take lessons from that rooster."

Do not waste your talents on someone who
lacks the taste to appreciate them.

The Boys *and the* Frogs

A fable of Aesop.

A group of boys who were playing at the edge of a pond soon began to throw rocks at the frogs who swam in the water. After several frogs had been killed, one frog poked its head above water and cried, "Stop your cruel sport! What is play to you is death to us."

The Soul-Taker

Adapted from an Armenian folktale.

Three sisters lived in the hills. They were kind and generous people of deep faith. One day they were digging in the backyard of their home and they uncovered a large box. They opened it up and discovered it was full of gold. All three began to scream, "Beware of the soul-taker! Whatever will we do? Do we bury it again, or do we simply have to leave our house?"

Four men who had recently moved into the house next door overheard the conversation. They walked to the home of the three sisters and inquired about their problem. "We are trying to decide how to get away from the soul-taker," they said.

"What is a soul-taker?" the small man asked. "Show us."

The sisters walked to the far corner of their lot and pointed at the box full of gold coins. "This is the soul-taker," they said.

The four men laughed. "Can you believe it?" the large one asked. "They think gold is a soul-taker." The others roared with laughter.

The bearded one spoke next, "If you women are frightened, go into town for a few hours and we'll take care of your problem."

The women agreed and left immediately.

The four men began to make plans. They decided to divide the gold equally. They also decided that two of them would go to the store to get something to eat, and the other two would finish digging up the box.

The two men who stayed to work agreed that things would be much better if they were able to split the gold two ways. They made plans to ambush and kill the other two when they returned and bury them in the hole where the box was found.

Meanwhile, the two men who went to buy the food also decided to divide the gold. "We'll poison the food," they said. "When the other two die, we'll bury them in the hole made by the box."

When they returned from the store, the men who stayed home ambushed and killed their companions. Before they buried the corpses they decided to eat the food while it was still fresh. Soon after they began to eat, they both got very sick and died.

When the three sisters returned to their home they saw four dead men and a box of gold. "We told them that it was a soul-taker, but they didn't believe us," the women said as they again left home to get away from the gold.

Four Quarters *of the* World

This is a Yiddish story.

A scholar was traveling on his way to give an important lecture when the rain began to fall in torrents. When the rain stopped, the river quickly rose above the bridge and the scholar was unable to cross. He hired a carpenter who owned a rowboat to take him to the other side.

As the carpenter prepared the boat, the scholar began a conversation. "Living this far from civilization, do you have access to a quality newspaper?" he asked the carpenter.

"I seldom read a newspaper at all. What news I get comes from radio and TV," the carpenter replied as he put the boat in the water.

"My dear man," the scholar said, "anyone who doesn't read a daily newspaper is deprived of a quarter of the world."

As he boarded the boat the scholar asked another question, "You do have a library nearby where you can check out good books, don't you?"

As he took the oars in his massive hands, the carpenter shook his head, "I haven't read a book in years."

"If you don't read good books, you waste another quarter of the world," the scholar said sadly. He paused for a moment and then spoke again, "What about plays and symphonies? Where do you see drama and listen to good music?"

Pulling hard against the current, the carpenter grunted, "I wouldn't mind going to plays and symphonies, but they are terribly expensive and are far away. I'm afraid what culture I get comes from TV."

The scholar was amazed. "Without drama and good music you waste another quarter of the world."

Just then the boat hit a stump and capsized. "Sir," the carpenter shouted, "can you swim?"

"No," the scholar shouted in fear.

"Well then, I figure you just wasted all four quarters of your world." Grabbing an oar he pushed it in front of the scholar. "Hang on to this and I'll pull you and your fancy world to safety."

Index of Biblical Texts

As indicated in the preface, a number of the stories in this book were based on specific biblical texts. These stories have been marked with an asterisk (*). The rest of stories, with one exception (#), have been collected and adapted by the author. These have been assigned a text. It will be clear that for a few of the stories, particularly in the concluding chapter, the relationship between story and biblical text is indirect.